GLOBETROTTER™

Travel Guide

S0-AHC-387

CAPE TOWN

PETER JOYCE

NEW HOLLAND

NEW
HOLLAND

★★★ Highly recommended
★★ Recommended
★ See if you can

Sixth edition published in 2008
by New Holland Publishers (UK) Ltd
London • Cape Town • Sydney • Auckland
First published in 1999
10 9 8 7 6 5 4 3 2 1

Website: www.newhollandpublishers.com

Garfield House,
86 Edgware Road
London W2 2EA
United Kingdom

80 McKenzie Street
Cape Town 8001
South Africa

Unit 1, 66 Gibbes Street
Chatswood, NSW 2067
Australia

218 Lake Road
Northcote, Auckland
New Zealand

ISBN 978 1 84537 964 3

Keep us Current
Information in travel guides is apt to change, which is why
we regularly update our guides. We'd be grateful to receive
feedback if you've noted something we should include in
our updates. If you have new information, please share it
with us by writing to the Publishing Manager, Globetrotter,
at the office nearest to you (addresses on this page). The
most significant contribution to each new edition will
receive a free copy of the updated guide.

Publishing Manager: Thea Grobbelaar
DTP Cartographic Manager: Genené Hart
Editors: Thea Grobbelaar, Alicha van Reenen, Melany
McCallum, Tarryn Berry, Sean Fraser, Gill Gordon,
Nune Jordaan
Cover Design: Nicole Bannister
Design and DTP: Lellyn Creamer, Lyndall Hamilton
Cartographers: Carryck Wise, Elmari Kuyler, Marisa
Galloway, Nicole Bannister
Consultant: Sean Fraser
Reproduction by Hirt & Carter (Pty) Ltd, Cape Town
Printed and bound by Times Offset (M) Sdn. Bhd.,
Malaysia.

Photographic credits:
Africana Museum, page 13 (left); **Shaen Adey,** pages 38
(bottom), 41 (top), 54 [IOA], 99, 105 [IOA], 112, 114,
115; **Captour,** page 14; **Gerald Cubitt,** pages 4, 13 (far
right), 23 (top), 35, 38 (top), 39, 49 (bottom), 50, 55, 65,
77, 80 (bottom), 97, 98; **Pat de la Harpe,** page 101; **Roger de la
Harpe,** pages 42 (bottom), 47, 51; **Leonard Hoffman/IOA,**
pages 43, 60, 61, 88; **Walter Knirr,** pages 57, 64, 102,
113; **Anne Laing,** page 18; **Tertius Pickard** [Touchline
Photo], page 73; **Peter Pickford/IOA,** pages 44, 48, 68,
81, 86; **Alain Proust,** pages 36 (bottom), 92; **Peter Ribton,**
page 49 (top); **Darran Skibbe,** pages 9, 23 (bottom), 24, 25
(top), 29 (bottom), 40, 67; **Mark Skinner,** pages 26, 66;
Stephan Smith/IOA [www.stephansmith.co.za], cover;
Stans and Downing, page 22; **Images of Africa [IOA],**
pages 20, 21, 29 (top), 70, 78, 93, 106; **Janek
Szymanowski/IOA,** pages 31, 96; **Erhardt Thiel/IOA,**
pages 7, 8, 10, 12, 15, 17, 25 (bottom), 30, 32, 33, 34, 36
(top), 42 (top), 46, 52, 62, 72, 74 (top and bottom), 75,
76, 80 (top), 83, 84, 85, 89, 90 (bottom), 94, 110, 111;
Mark van Aardt, pages 11, 37, 41 (bottom), 58, 87 (left
and right), 100; *Courtesy of* **V&A Waterfront Company,**
pages 19, 116; **Keith Young,** title page, pages 53, 90 (top),
108, 109.
[IOA: Images of Africa, www.imagesofafrica.co.za]

Although every effort has been made to ensure that this
guide is up to date and current at time of going to print,
the Publisher accepts no responsibility or liability for any
loss, injury or inconvenience incurred by readers or
travellers using this guide.

Cover: *Colourful beach huts at Muizenberg.*
Title page: *Table Mountain floodlit.*

CONTENTS

1
Introducing
Cape Town

South Africa's 'Mother City', located at the southern tip of the continent, enjoys a matchless setting. Nestling snugly in the natural amphitheatre between the immensity of **Table Mountain** and the blue waters of **Table Bay**, it is a modern, cosmopolitan, stylishly attractive metropolis of graceful thoroughfares, handsome buildings and glittering shops – and it is fast becoming one of the southern hemisphere's premier tourist destinations.

Cape Town is a rather small city by world standards. The central area, its growth confined by both sea and mountain, covers just a small area. But the wider metropolitan area is enormous: the main thrust of development has been suburban, and the suburbs seem to go on for ever, each one a village or modest-sized town in its own right. To travel between, say, the western coastal centres of Kommetjie and Atlantis involves an 80km (50-mile) journey.

The city proper occupies the northern part of the **Cape Peninsula**, a 54km-long (34-mile) scenic finger of land that ends, dramatically, in the towering headland known as **Cape Point**. Popular belief has it that this is the division between the cold waters of the **Atlantic** and the warm waters of the **Indian Ocean** – a common misconception, since the technical separation takes places much further east, off the coast of **Cape Agulhas**, Africa's southernmost extremity. Nevertheless there are striking differences of character and mood between the Peninsula's flanking seas. Visitors expecting

Don't Miss

*** **Table Mountain:** a world-famous landmark.
*** **Cape Point:** at the southern tip of the Peninsula.
*** **Victoria and Alfred Waterfront:** historic dockland area transformed into a shopping and dining mecca.
*** **Wine routes:** in the lovely Constantia valley and vineyards of the hinterland.
*** **The Castle:** formidable, built to defend the colony.
*** **Century City** and **GrandWest:** for shoppers and gamblers.

Opposite: *The Mother City, nestled invitingly between mountain and bay.*

WORLD HERITAGE

The Cape Peninsula, stretching from Signal Hill to Cape Point, and including Table Mountain, was declared a national park in May 1998. The Table Mountain National Park (previously the Cape Peninsula National Park) covers approximately 30,000ha (74,000 acres) of both state and privately owned land, and includes within its protectorate thousands of animal and plant species – including the *fynbos* of the unique Cape Floral Kingdom, a World Heritage Site.

conventional images of the Dark Continent will be disappointed. There is nothing of the classical Africa about Cape Town and its surrounds – no heat-hazed veld stretching to far horizons, no distant drumbeats, no wild animals circling the bounds of your safari camp. The city is too old, the region too well settled, and the countryside too green and gentle to sustain such romantic notions.

But there are other powerful attractions: a near-perfect Mediterranean climate, landscapes that delight the eye, spectacular beaches, the grandeur of **Table Mountain**, the exuberant **Waterfront** development, fine hotels, a myriad eating and drinking places, a lively and entertaining calendar of arts, and an enchanting wineland-and-mountain hinterland.

THE LAND

Much of the Peninsula comprises a well-watered, green-mantled sandstone plateau that reaches its most spectacular heights in the great bulk of **Table Mountain** itself. Two distinctively shaped features, **Devil's Peak** and **Lion's Head**, stand sentry to either side of the massif. Defining the plateau's western rim is a series of imposing buttresses known as the **Twelve Apostles** (there are in fact 18 of them).

The shoreline is an entrancing combination of bay and white sand, high cliff and secluded cove. Inland are wooded valleys of magical beauty. To the north and east are the **Cape**

Cape Peninsula

Left: *Strandfontein beach and, stretching to the horizon, the sandy plain known as the Cape Flats.*

Left: *Strandfontein beach and, stretching to the horizon, the sandy plain known as the Cape Flats.*

INVADERS FROM OZ

Perhaps the most aggressive of the alien plants that endanger the Peninsula's unique indigenous flora is the **Port Jackson** willow, a hardy perennial tree that is native to **Australia**. These plants were brought in during the 1840s to stabilize the **Cape Flats** – the low, sandy area to the northeast of the city that the early Dutch settlers knew as *Die Groote Woeste Vlakte*, ('The Great Desolate Plain') for its nightmare of drifting dunes. The species adapted very well and it spread virulently over the wider region. It propagates quickly, and its hard, deep roots make clearing difficult and expensive.

Flats – a low, sandy flatland that once, not too long ago on the geophysical timetable, lay beneath the sea. Their shifting dunes proved a formidable obstacle to early Dutch colonists on their way inland, but the sands were eventually stabilized (with exotic vegetation that spread rapidly and today threatens the indigenous flora) and are now heavily populated.

Beyond lie the hills, vineyards, orchards and lush pastures of the famed **Cape Winelands**.

Climate

Cape Town falls within the winter-rainfall belt, its climate **Mediterranean** in character. Weather patterns are complex and conditions variable – at times the city seems to pass through all four seasons in a single 24-hour period – but generally the summers are hot, sunny and very dry. The heat can be oppressive, especially when the warm 'berg wind' blows in from the interior. More often the air is cooled by a gusty, unnerving and sometimes violent (or 'black') southeaster that may reach gale force and last for a week or even longer. The

CAPE TOWN	J	F	M	A	M	J	J	A	S	O	N	D
AVERAGE TEMP. °C	21	21	20	17	15	13	12	13	14	16	18	20
AVERAGE TEMP. °F	70	70	69	63	58	55	54	55	57	61	64	68
HOURS OF SUN DAILY	11	10	9	7	6	6	6	7	8	9	10	11
SEA TEMP. °C	15	14	13	13	12	12	12	13	13	14	14	14
SEA TEMP. °F	59	57	55	55	54	54	54	55	55	57	57	57
RAINFALL mm	14	17	19	39	74	92	70	75	39	37	15	17
RAINFALL in	1	1	1	2	3	4	3	3	2	2	1	1
DAYS OF RAINFALL	5	4	5	8	12	12	11	13	10	8	5	5

Above: *A blustery start to the prestigious South Atlantic Race. Cape Town features prominently on the international sailing calendar.*

The **cycads** on view at **Kirstenbosch** are immensely ancient seed-bearing plants that date back more than 200 million years – to the time when the dinosaurs ruled the earth, and before the advent of flowering species. Though they look rather like palms, they are in fact relatives of the conifers. Two genera are indigenous to South Africa: *Encephalartos*, to which 28 species belong, and the single-species *Stangeria*. Cycads are strictly protected but, because of their rarity and high export value, remain vulnerable to illegal traders. Smugglers face stiff penalties.

wind is commonly known as the **Cape Doctor** for its supposedly cleansing effect on the city (there may have been some truth in this in the early days when epidemic-type diseases were quite common at the Cape).

Winter is known as the **green season**. The moist, prevailing wind from the northwest brings damp chill and driving rain, and snow to the mountains of the coastal rampart. The long, cold, wet spells, though, are invariably broken by brief and delightfully unexpected intervals of warmth and welcome sunshine.

Cape Town is an attractive place to visit at any time of the year; each of the months has its appeal. Perhaps the best months are those from high summer through to early winter (January to May), when the sun falls ever more kindly on the face, and the suburbs and countryside begin to take on the lovely, rustic colours of autumn.

Plant Life

The region's natural heritage is both unique and fascinating. Indigenous vegetation largely comprises the *fynbos* ('fine bush') of the **Cape Floral Kingdom**, a zone which extends over the southern coastal belt and contains about 8500 different species. Of these, some 2600 are found on the Peninsula itself.

The zone accounts for a minuscule 0.04% of the earth's land area and yet, because it is so rich in its floral diversity, it is ranked as one of the world's six major botanical divisions, enjoying equal status with the vast Boreal Kingdom encompassing the whole of North America and most of Europe and Asia.

Most of the plants are low-growing and hardy, well adapted to withstand the summertime droughts.

Some are quite lovely; the more prominent include the **proteas**, more than 600 different kinds of **erica** (heath), the reed-like **restios**, the **lilies**, **orchids**, **red-hot pokers** and **disas**. An especially charming member of this last group is *Disa uniflora*, the 'Pride of Table Mountain'. The tallest of the family proteaceae is the **silver tree** (*Leucadendron argenteum*), which grows to more than 10m (33ft) and whose silver-green leaves, covered in silky-haired down, shimmer entrancingly in the breeze.

Around 80% of the different plant types are confined to particular areas of the Kingdom, some even to micro-habitats of just a few square metres, and this renders them especially vulnerable to human encroachment. It has been reckoned that more than 1500 species are threatened with extinction.

CITY PROFILE

Cape Town is the country's fourth largest urban centre and oldest city, founded in the mid-1600s to serve as a halfway station between Holland and its Far Eastern possessions. For centuries it was known as the **Tavern of the Seas**, drawing much of its prosperity from its harbour.

Maritime traffic has declined over the past few decades and the **harbour**, second in size only to

The Western Cape is home to most of South Africa's 368 species of protea (named after Proteus, a mythological Greek god who could change his shape at will). Among the best-known proteas are the **sugarbush** (*Protea repens*), the **waboom** (or wagon-tree, *Protea nitida*), which grows to 7m (23ft), and the **king protea** (*Protea cynaroides*), which has the largest and most attractive flowers of all the species and is South Africa's national flower.

• Cape Town's harbour is the second biggest after Durban's; the dry dock is the country's largest.
• The city lies at the south-western tip of the African continent, 1402km (871 miles) from Johannesburg in the north, 1753km (1089 miles) from Durban in the east, and 769km (478 miles) from Port Elizabeth along the southern coast.
• The Western Cape's total population is over 4.5 million.
• The highest point within the metropolitan area is Maclear's Beacon on Table Mountain, 1087m (3566ft) above sea level.

Left: *Adderley Street, with buildings old and new.*

Durban's, is a lot quieter than it was in the heyday of the great East Indiamen sailing ships and, later, the passenger steamers.

Still, Cape Town remains a major port city. **Ship repair** is a thriving industry; the dry dock is the southern hemisphere's largest. Mercantile enterprises contribute a lot to a local economy that also embraces **marine fisheries**, **petroleum refining**, light (and increasingly high-tech) **engineering**, **manufacturing** (notably clothing and textiles), **banking**, **insurance** and other services – and, of course, **tourism** is a rapidly expanding industry.

The metropolitan area, recently consolidated within what's known as the 'unicity', extends southwards, along the suburban railway line, through Observatory, Mowbray, Rondebosch, Newlands, Wynberg (these are the oldest of the suburbs, founded as colonial farms in the 17th century) to the historic naval centre of Simon's Town, near Cape Point. The fashionable western or 'Atlantic' suburbs are closer to the city; affluent and semirural Constantia occupies much of the central Peninsula. The northern and eastern (Cape Flats) areas are dense with industrial and residential development that includes, among much else, Bellville, which gained city status in the 1970s; the fairly new town of Mitchell's Plain; great swathes of high-density housing (including the townships of Langa, Nyanga, Gugulethu and Khayelitsha) and some big, ultramodern mall complexes.

HISTORY IN BRIEF

Cape Town was born on 6 April 1652 when Commander Jan van Riebeeck led his small party of Dutch settlers ashore to establish a replenishment station for the

THE CRUEL SEA

Over the centuries more than 1300 ships have been wrecked along South Africa's rocky coasts, many of them off the 'Cape of Storms'. In the great gale of 1865 no less than 11 vessels sank in Table Bay alone. Numerous others foundered on or close to the coasts (**Shipwreck and Lighthouse Route**; details from Cape Town Tourism). Among the many sea-related tales of tragedy and heroism is that of Wolraad Woltemade, who braved the ocean seven times to rescue survivors from *De Jonge Thomas*, wrecked in the bay in June 1773. On the eighth trip, both he and his horse disappeared beneath the waves. The Woltemade Decoration has ranked as South Africa's highest civilian honour for gallantry.

Indies-bound trading fleets of the **Dutch East India Company's** great maritime empire.

At that time, and for generations before, the Peninsula was home to groups of **Khoikhoi** (Hottentots), semi-nomadic, cattle-owning people related to the **San** (Bushmen) hunter-gatherers of the interior.

Van Riebeeck's instructions were to cultivate friendly relations with the local inhabitants – to whom, after all, the countryside belonged. The colonists needed fresh meat, the Khoikhoi were keen to barter, and for the most part the two cultures managed to coexist in reasonable harmony. Later, rivalry for grazing land and trading rights was to lead to open conflict.

The Early Years

The settlers were determined to make their outpost self-sufficient. Their prime tasks were 'to erect defences, and to secure herbs, flesh, water and other needful refreshments'.

Within days of landing Van Riebeeck had marked out the site of a fort, and before the end of April the first walls were up and supporting five cannons. There were plenty of setbacks – the Cape rainstorms played havoc with the earthen ramparts – but the structure served its purpose well enough for 20-odd years. In due course it was to be replaced by a splendid, new five-sided bastion known as **The Castle**, today South Africa's oldest occupied building. After an initial struggle with the elements, the newcomers also established the **Company's Garden**; a flourishing vegetable farm, now a public garden. Over the years its rows of humble plants gave way to more decorative features – lemon and fruit trees, an avenue of oaks, a pleasure lodge (now **De Tuynhuys**, the state president's city office), the **Iziko Slave Lodge** (which functions as part of the cultural history museum; see page 30),

see page 30

THE EARLIEST EXPLORERS

The 15th-century Portuguese navigators were not the first to see Africa's southernmost shores. Some 2000 years earlier, Phoenician galleys almost certainly rounded the Cape, although unlike later voyagers they sailed down the east coast. They had been sent by the pharaoh, Necho, to pass Zanzibar and return 'through the Pillars of Hercules' (Gibraltar). According to Greek historian Herodotus, the Phoenicians reported that, in sailing around Libya (the ancient name for Africa), they 'had the sun on their right hand'. So, they had travelled westwards past Cape Point!

Opposite: *The harbour is among the southern hemisphere's biggest.*
Below: *The Castle of Good Hope is the most enduring of the buildings erected by early European settlers.*

The first **Cape** slaves arrived in 1657, from **Angola** and **West Africa**. Later, they were brought in from the **Dutch** possessions of the **Indies**. Those assigned to work in town were rather better off than their country cousins: they were lodged in the slave quarters (now the Cultural History Museum), and provided with regular meals and schooling for their children. Some skilled slaves, who could hire themselves out as artisans, earned enough to buy their freedom.

Below: *The historic Iziko South African Museum flanking the Company's Garden.*

a menagerie (now an aviary), and an area set aside for the cultivation of rare plants – a role the garden still fulfils with honour. Today it is much smaller than it was then – buildings have encroached on three sides – but remains as lovely as ever.

During the first years, other basics of civic life made their appearance: hospital, jetty, simple houses, a scatter of public buildings. Most imposing of the latter was the high-steepled, thatched and gabled **Groote Kerk**, the Dutch Reformed (Calvinist) mother church, erected in 1704. Linking the shoreline – which at that time ran through what is now the city centre – with the Company's Garden was the elegant, stone-paved, oak-lined **Heerengracht** (translating roughly as 'Gentlemen's walk along the canal'), renamed **Adderley Street** during the late 19th century. The section below the fountain, currently named the Heerengracht, is part of the land (Foreshore) that was reclaimed from the sea in the 1930s.

Other prominent features of early 18th-century Cape Town included a spacious **Grand Parade** flanking the Castle; Greenmarket Square, the town's commercial hub, and some fine private homes built in the evolving and increasingly beautiful Cape Dutch style. Special among the latter was **Koopmans-De Wet House** on Strand Street. By the time the British displaced the Dutch at the end

of the 18th century, Cape Town had grown into an elegant little place, one of the southern hemisphere's busiest ports and host to ships and sailors from a dozen nations. Its population comprised about 6000 Europeans and several thousand more people of Malay and mixed-descent stock, many of them slaves or descendants of slaves. Suburbs had crept up the lower slopes of Table

Left: *Charming Adderley Street in the 1830s.*
Above: *Harvesting Cape wines, which are fast gaining worldwide recognition.*

Mountain, and a chain of rural centres, leading from Woodstock to Simon's Town, had gone a long way towards taming the Peninsula.

Spirit of the Vine

From the earliest years the settlers began importing much-needed labour for a settlement that was expanding, not only through the Peninsula but into the hinterland.

Prompted by the need to feed the colony, men had been released from Company employment to establish farms, and during the 1660s they began infiltrating the traditional Khoikhoi lands of the interior. **Stellenbosch**, 48km (30 miles) northeast of Cape Town, was founded in 1679 and thereafter valley after valley was occupied, the countryside turned over to pasture, wheat and the growing of wine grapes.

In fact the first vines had been planted by Van Riebeeck himself in 1655, to yield 'mainly muscadel and other white round grapes of truly fine bouquet and taste'. The long-serving (1679–99) and able Governor Simon van der Stel also showed a very keen interest in **viticulture**, devoting some of his boundless energy and part of his gracious **Groot Constantia** property, south of Table Mountain, to vineyards. The excellent Constantia wines were eventually to find their

THE FIRST VINTAGE

The Western Cape's flourishing **wine industry** has its origins in the very first year of white settlement. Just a month after stepping ashore in April 1652, **Jan van Riebeeck** asked his masters in Amsterdam for 'vines which ought to thrive as well on these hill slopes as they do in Spain and France'. In due course 12,000 were growing on his private farm, and in 1659 he was able to confide to his journal that 'today, praise be to God, wine can be made for the first time from Cape grapes, namely from the new must fresh from the vat'. Well before the end of the century grapes were being harvested around the young country towns of **Stellenbosch**, **Franschhoek** and **Paarl**.

Opposite: *The Mount Nelson Hotel, gracious host to a who's who of notables for the past century.*
Below: *A rare plate bearing the monogram of the Dutch East India Company.*

way onto the aristocratic tables of Europe. The arrival in 1688 of a small group of **French Huguenots** – Protestant refugees from Europe's religious wars – gave impetus to the fledgling industry. By 1690 half a million vines were flourishing on the Peninsula and in the winelands around Stellenbosch.

The British Occupation

For more than two centuries Cape Town functioned as the centre of a growing colony that, under the Dutch, pushed its frontiers 800km (500 miles) eastwards, through the lands of the Xhosa as far as the Great Fish River.

With the decline of the Netherlands towards the end of the 18th century, the British first took control of the Cape in 1795, and some time later withdrew from the colony for about eight years. They returned, however, in 1806 and the territory became a **Crown Colony** in 1814, progressing first to representative government (1854) and finally to full self-government (1872) with a constitution modelled on the two-chamber Westminster system. The vote was based on income and property rather than on race – a concession to democracy that the apartheid politicians later withdrew. A high commissioner was appointed to look after British interests and, with **Union** in 1910, the colony became one of the country's four provinces, with Cape Town designated the nation's legislative capital.

Growing Up

Around the middle of the 1800s Cape Town's population stood at a modest 24,000, but the latter half of the century brought rapid growth, fuelled by revenue from the fabulous **Kimberley** diamond fields far to the north and from the city's ever-busier harbour.

The first tarred road was laid in the 1850s (timber paving had previously been tried, but proved too slippery), as was the inaugural railway line – between

Adderley Street and the Winelands town of Wellington. The original locomotive, built in 1859 in Scotland and shipped out for assembly, is on view in the main station concourse. Horse-drawn trams were introduced in 1863, initially operating between the city and the ocean suburb of Sea Point. The first motor car took to the streets in 1895, and a year later the electric tram heralded the demise of the horse as Cape Town's principal means of transport.

By the end of the century the central area had developed beyond recognition, and Cape Town had acquired its own, unique character as the 'gateway to Africa'. Ships' chandlers did a roaring trade, Union Castle mailships regularly offloaded cargoes of immigrants, seamen from a score of far-flung lands haunted the taverns and lodging houses, and attractive hotels catered for the more well-to-do visitors. Among these was the grand new Mount Nelson Hotel, which hosted a veritable who's who of Britain during the Anglo-Boer War (1899–1902), including a young, dashing Winston Churchill, of London's *Morning Post*.

The city was equally hospitable during World War II, when it welcomed troopships bound for the Far East theatre.

Today Cape Town is of course much bigger and – because the apartheid years brought so much human deprivation and suffering – less complacent, more socially and economically unstable. But the core personality and charm with which it has become associated remains. The Mother City is still very much in the hospitality business, beckoning the traveller, entertaining him well, and sending him on his way with pleasant memories.

PAGE OF THE MUSEUMS

Iziko Museums is a group of 14 prime places of interest, with five major components. Ring (021) 481-3800 for information. Venues include:
★★★ The Castle, Buitenkant Street: the oldest occupied building in the country.
★★★ Iziko Slave Lodge, Adderley Street: part of the Cultural History Museum complex.
★★★ Groot Constantia, Constantia Valley: elegant Cape Dutch mansion, wine museum, cellar tours.
★★ Iziko South African Museum, Queen Victoria Street: geology, archaeology, natural history.
★★ Koopmans-De Wet House, Strand Street: elegant and historic period house. Among notable independent venues are the Simon's Town Museum (naval history and much else) and the Rugby Museum in Newlands, largest of its kind in the world.

HISTORICAL CALENDAR

Pre-colonial era Cape Peninsula and hinterland occupied by groups of Khoikhoi (Hottentots), semi-nomadic, cattle-owning people who over the centuries had competed with and largely displaced aboriginal San (Bushmen) hunter-gatherers as the region's dominant human presence.

1460–1510 The age of Portuguese exploration: navigators chart sea route to India. Dias rounds Cape in 1488; Da Gama reaches India in 1498; De Saldanha sails into Table Bay and climbs Table Mountain in 1503; D'Almeida killed in battle with Khoikhoi in 1510, after which the Portuguese lose interest.

1580 English admiral Drake sights 'the fairest Cape in all the circumference of the earth'.

1595–1647 Dutch East India Company fleets explore coast, trade with Khoikhoi.

1652 Dutch party under Jan van Riebeeck establishes Cape settlement.

1657 First white farmers settle the land. First slaves imported.

1659 First serious conflict between Khoikhoi and white colonists. First wine produced.

1660s Explorers make their way inland, and along south and west coasts.

1671 Second settler-Khoikhoi war.

1679 Castle of Good Hope completed. The enlightened Simon van der Stel appointed Cape commander (later governor); Stellenbosch founded.

1685 Slaves granted right to buy their freedom.

1713 First great smallpox epidemic devastates Khoikhoi community; more epidemics in 1755 and 1767.

1780–83 War between Holland and Britain hastens demise of Dutch East India Co, in decline since 1750s. Cape Town hosts French troops (Holland's allies).

1795–1803 First British occupation of the Cape.

1798 Much of Cape Town destroyed by fire.

1803 Cape reverts to Dutch rule.

1806 Second British occupation.

1814 Cape formally ceded to Britain.

1829 South African College (now University of Cape Town) founded.

1834 Slavery abolished.

1859–60 Work starts on first railway line (to Wellington) and on Table Bay docks.

1869 Kimberley diamonds discovered; Cape Town enters new age of growth and prosperity.

1872 Cape Colony gains responsible government.

1879 Cape Town and London linked by cable.

1881 First electric lighting installed.

1890 Cecil Rhodes becomes Cape premier.

1892 Cape Town to Johannesburg railway line officially inaugurated.

1899–1902 Anglo-Boer War; Cape Town accommodates British forces.

1910 Cape Town becomes legislative capital of unified South Africa.

1918 Influenza epidemic kills thousands.

1925 Prince of Wales visits city.

1926 First motor-powered mailship arrives at Table Bay.

1939–45 City welcomes Allied troops.

1947 British royal family visits Cape Town.

1956 The Coloured people of the country lose their parliamentary vote.

1957 The British Royal Navy relinquishes Simon's Town naval base.

1960 British premier Macmillan delivers 'wind of change' address to parliament in Cape Town.

1963 Nelson Mandela imprisoned 'for life'.

1966 District Six declared a 'white' area; removal of Coloured residents begins. South African prime minister Verwoerd assassinated.

1967 Christiaan Barnard performs world's first heart transplant at Groote Schuur Hospital.

1970s and 1980s Liberation struggle gains momentum; mounting unrest in townships.

1990 Mandela released from prison; addresses huge crowd on Grand Parade.

1994 First democratic elections. President Nelson Mandela opens historic parliament in Cape Town.

1999 Nelson Mandela resigns presidency, and is succeeded by Thabo Mbeki.

2003 Cape Town International Convention Centre (CTICC) opens.

2003 Truth and Reconciliation Council ends after seven years of testimony.

2004 Ten years of democracy.

Left: *The colourful Minstrel Carnival enlivens the city's streets each New Year.*

MUSIC OF THE STREETS

The **Cape Coloured** community has a lively musical tradition, drawn from a rich cultural heritage. Although the origins of many of the *ghomma*-style songs are obscure, the cheerful and sometimes racy words and melodies are still heard at gatherings. The **Minstrel Carnival** is a wonderfully animated New Year street festival of music and dance that owes much to the emancipation of the slaves and the abolition of slavery in 1834. On this annual occasion, brightly costumed bands mass together on the **Grand Parade** before making their way along the thoroughfares to **Green Point.**

THE PEOPLE

Greater Cape Town's population totals well over three million, a figure that will rise by another million and more within the next decade if the present pattern of 'urban drift' continues.

Ethnic origins cover the racial and cultural spectrum, from old **Dutch**, **Cape-Afrikaner** and **English-Colonial** families to penniless, destitute shack-dwellers from rural Transkei. The area was, until 1994, an 'independent homeland' but is now incorporated into the province of the Eastern Cape.

Largest of the 'groups' – a much looser term now than in the bad old days of segregation – is the mixed-descent or **Coloured**, a society with diverse roots. It is largely Afrikaans-speaking (though most are fluent in English, spoken with a lilting accent), largely Christian and wholly Westernized in lifestyle and custom. It does, however, have a distinctive and joyous musical tradition. On New Year's Day sections of the community put on the **Minstrel Carnival**, an exuberant and marvellously colourful parade through the city's streets. The Coloured people were a more or less integrated

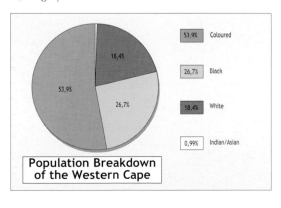

53,9% Coloured
26,7% Black
18,4% White
0,99% Indian/Asian

Population Breakdown of the Western Cape

THE SWORD DANCE

Among the more dramatic of **Cape Muslim** traditions is the *Ratiep*, a sword dance, led by a 'master of ceremonies' (*Khalifa*). It was performed under a self-induced trance during which young men pierced their flesh with swords and other sharp instruments. Remarkably, this did not draw blood, and left no wound. Today the ritual has lost its religious relevance and in fact many of the *imams* (spiritual leaders), frown on the practice, though it still takes place as an occasional spectacle.

Below: *Happy faces sporting the South African flag in celebration of a Springbok rugby victory.*

part of Cape society until the 1950s when, after some cynical tampering with the constitution, the government removed their voting rights. A decade later many also lost their homes: the renowned District Six inner suburb was demolished and its residents moved to the bleakness of the Cape Flats (*see* panel, page 35).

A prominent subgroup are the 200,000 **Cape Muslims**, whose forefathers came, as slaves, from the Indonesian islands and other eastern regions. They were valued for their skills as craftsmen (and for their wonderful cuisine; *see* page 20). Many who were not originally of the faith converted to Islam on arrival. Among the newcomers were high-born political exiles – men such as Sheik Yusuf, who had led a rebellion against the Dutch in Java. With the abolition of slavery in the 1830s, a fair number of these highly respected people settled in the picturesque Bo-Kaap ('Upper Cape Town', known as the Malay Quarter) on the slopes of Signal Hill, on the city's western perimeter. There was little intermarriage with other groups, and it has remained a highly integrated, devout community. Its members attend their city mosques, and many make pilgrimages, not only to Mecca (as is required of all Muslims who can afford the journey) but to the local *kramats*, or tombs of the holy men. Among the more eye-catching of ancient traditions to survive is the *Ratiep*, a trance-induced sword dance that once played a part in religious ceremony. It is still sometimes performed in the Cape (*see* side panel).

The majority of Cape Town's black citizens are migrants or the descendants of migrants from the historic **Xhosa** 'homelands' of the Eastern Cape. Most live on the Cape Flats, in the sprawling suburbs of Langa, Nyanga, Gugulethu and Khayelitsha and the surrounding informal settlements; many in appalling conditions.

Left: *Inside one of the Waterfront's restaurants. The leisure area, comprising the old harbour's Victoria and Alfred docks, is a glittering, and rapidly growing, tourist mecca.*

The black people of the region have inherited a harsh legacy. Under the apartheid regime the south-western Cape was deemed a 'Coloured preference area', and if you were a black person you couldn't get a job or a place to live, and you faced repatriation.

Forced removals did not halt the influx. Poor people continued to pour in from a countryside that could no longer meet their minimum needs. And because they were 'illegal', very little provision was made for them in the way of houses, schools, clinics, roads and services.

South Africa is now a democratic country, movement is no longer restricted, and a lot of money is being invested in upliftment. But huge backlogs remain in the Cape and elsewhere, and these issues definitely pose the greatest challenge of the future.

Food and Drink

Cape Town's myriad restaurants offer the full range of food styles – from the classic to the exotic. Areas with especially heavy concentrations of eateries are the new big mall and leisure developments in the northern areas (*see page 56*), the Victoria & Alfred Waterfront, and the southern suburban stretch from Rondebosch through to Claremont.

The local **line fish**, **rock lobster** (crayfish) and **abalone** (*perlemoen*) are usually excellent, though the **shellfish**

THE GAY LIFE

The national constitution protects the rights of gays and lesbians; Cape Town is regarded as the country's 'gay capital'. Publications include the *Pink Map* and *Cape Town Gay Guide*; bookshops stock *OUTRight, Exit, Women on Women* and other periodicals, including the *Cape Review* and *South African City Life*. There's also the **Gay Lesbian and Bisexual Helpline**, tel: (021) 448-3812, and the **Pink Travel Desk** in the Gay Village, Green Point, tel: (021) 425-6461, www.cape infoafrica.co.za These sources yield detailed information on the city's gay-friendly venues and activities – shops, restaurants, bars, guesthouses, B&Bs, night-spots, film, video and cabaret shows. Annual events include the **Mother City Queer Project party** (Dec) and the **film festival** (Jan/Feb).

tends to be expensive. Sushi and Thai restaurants are also abundant. Antelope **venison** (including springbok pie) is something of a speciality, and **ostrich** steaks are an increasingly popular menu item.

Old Cape **country fare**, available in selected restaurants, evolved among the rural Afrikaner communities. Common ingredients of the meal include tender Karoo lamb, sweet potatoes, cinnamon-flavoured pumpkin, sweetcorn fritters and, for dessert, milk tart, *koeksisters* and a selection of sticky preserves known as *konfyt*, all washed down with fragrant *rooibos* tea, made from the leaves of an indigenous herbal bush.

Rather tastier and less stodgy is **Malay cuisine**, introduced by the early slaves from Indonesia and famed for its aromatic *boboties* (curried meatloaf topped with savoury custard), *bredies* (fragrant stews, usually of mutton, potatoes and vegetables, although *waterblommetjie bredie* is a piquant variety made from a type of indigenous water lilies), spicy *samoosas* and gooey desserts. The traditional style has been refined over the centuries, taking on elements of early Dutch, French Huguenot and Indian cooking.

Opposite: *Typical Cape fare – kebabs, 'potjie' and 'pap'*
Right: *A traditional Cape Malay feast.*

Outdoor entertainment in Cape Town invariably centres around the *braai* or *braaivleis* – a standard barbecue of long-marinated lamb, venison, beef, chicken, spicy *boerewors* ('farmer's sausage'), with salads, and potatoes baked in foil. The men invariably do the cooking, which is considered something of an art form. Charcoal, wood or both are used for fuel, the wood imparting a distinctive and tasty flavour to the food.

Also popular is *potjiekos*: a flavourful stew cooked gently for hours and even days in a giant cast-iron pot over an open fire.

Traditional **African cuisine** does not yet appear on many menus, but this is changing, as innovative chefs introduce elements of African cuisine to their dishes. For most black people, eating remains a practical necessity; the ordinary meal of the day in the townships tends to be a no-nonsense affair in which maize-meal (*pap*), boiled meat or cabbage, or *samp* and beans is the order of the day. But living standards are slowly improving.

There are some 4000 locally produced wines on the market, from delicate dry whites to full-bodied reds. All are drinkable, many are noteworthy, a few truly memorable and the better ones are fast gaining an international reputation. The best way to explore the range is to embark on one or more of the world-famous wine routes (*see page 79*). Bookshops and some liquor stores stock informative guides to the wine-growing areas and the many labels on offer.

Entertainment and the Arts

Theatre and **music** are alive and doing well in Cape Town. The grander shows – drama, opera, ballet, oratorio and the occasional lavish musical – are staged at the **Artscape (Nico Theatre Centre)** on the Foreshore. The centre's three auditoriums are venues for an increasing number of international (imported) shows.

Popular plays, music and, sometimes, local and experimental drama can be enjoyed at the **Baxter Theatre Complex** (on Main Road, Rondebosch), whose two main halls each have a 600-plus capacity. There's also a small studio/workshop.

Some excellent professional productions – especially light musical and comic fare – are staged in Camps Bay's **Theatre on the Bay.** There are also a number of smaller, intimate theatres: check the press for up-to-date details.

Cape Town caters for most tastes in classical music. Evening concerts are often performed in ornately Baroque surrounds at the **City Hall**. Among other especially pleasant summertime venues are the Victoria and Alfred Waterfront's open-air **Amphitheatre**, the **Kirstenbosch** gardens in Newlands and, further afield, **Spier Wine Estate** and the **Oude Libertas Centre** in Stellenbosch.

There's plenty of live entertainment – jazz, pop, cabaret – on the night-time scene. Venues and performers change all the time; consult the local newspapers, Cape Town Tourism or Leisure and Entertainment Guides which are available from major bookshops. Most of the bigger hotels also offer dinner-dancing.

Sport and Recreation

There are some exquisite **beaches** along the Peninsula's shoreline and up the coast towards Bloubergstrand. Those on the western or 'Atlantic' side are sheltered from the prevailing summer wind, but the sea is rather cold for

SUN, SEA AND SAND

- **Bloubergstrand:** North of the city; offers safe bathing and fine views of Table Mountain.
- **Milnerton:** 8km (5 miles) of white sand and a large lagoon.
- **Peninsula west coast:** This long stretch of coastline between **Sea Point** and **Camps Bay**, known as the 'Cape Riviera', is especially attractive. **Clifton** has four fashionable beaches. Also close by are **Maiden's Cove** (for skin diving), **Glen Beach** (for surfing) and **Camps Bay** (for sunbathing). **Llandudno** is scenically beautiful; **Sandy Bay** is for all-over tanning.
- **Table Mountain National Park** has several pleasant and safe spots; **Maclear** beach is excellent for scuba diving and bathing.
- **Peninsula east coast:** **Muizenberg** has a long and beautiful beach; **St James** has a sheltered tidal pool, and **Boulders** has safe bathing and a penguin sanctuary.

comfortable bathing. On the other hand, False Bay in the east tends to be breezy but water temperatures are about 5°C (41°F) warmer and reach about 23°C (73°F) in summer. Visitors should stick to popular areas – those monitored by beach constables and life-savers – rather than seek seclusion. You'll find especially attractive stretches of beach

at Clifton and next-door Camps Bay, close to town, and at Muizenberg on the east coast. Noordhoek, in the west, is ideal for an early-morning **horseback ride**.

The rockier coves beckon the snorkeller and scuba diver. There are strict limits for fish, rock lobster and mollusc catches, and permits can be purchased at any post office. Rock and surf fishermen reel in snoek (barracouta), steenbras, red roman and kabeljou (kob). A number of companies offer game-fishing charters and game-fishing enthusiasts take marlin, swordfish and three species of tunny (tuna). A number of companies offer **game-fishing** charters. Because the sea is easily accessible from almost anywhere in the Peninsula, opportunities for **yachting, power-boating, board-sailing, waterskiing, parasailing** and other aquatic sports are limitless. For those who prefer more structured **swimming**, public pools are located in Sea Point (sea water), in the city at the top of Long Street (indoor, heated), and in Newlands (Olympic size); and smaller municipal pools in the suburbs.

The Peninsula is fine **walking** country; prime areas are the more secluded stretches of coastline, the hills and valleys inland, and, of course, the slopes of Table Mountain itself. There are five excellent walking routes up Table Mountain (*see page 41*).

Above: *The white sands of Clifton's popular and fashionable Fourth Beach.*
Opposite: *Artscape, focal point of the city's performing arts.*
Below: *The beautiful Cape Peninsula is ideal for hiking.*

Cape Town is one of the few South African cities whose central area is best explored on foot – much of what there is to see is within easy strolling distance. A word of caution: South Africa has been undergoing something of a social upheaval, poverty is everywhere and free-spending tourists are vulnerable to street

Right: *Hiking and rock climbing opportunities are plentiful on the mountains of the Cape.*

BEST WALKS

*** **City centre** and **Waterfront:** historical routes; booklets available from Cape Town Tourism.
*** **Table Mountain:** offers numerous walks and climbs; excellent guidebooks available at bookshops, including the Table Mountain Activity Guide and Best Walks in the Cape Peninsula.
*** **Table Mountain National Park:** there are many trails.
*** **Kirstenbosch National Botanical Gardens:** for the lover of plants and scenic splendour. Very relaxing.
** **Hout Bay:** several routes through beautiful hiking and rambling countryside – booklets and guide books available from Cape Town Tourism, Hout Bay.
** **Cecilia forest:** fringing the enchanting Constantia Valley. Easy walks.
** **Silvermine:** an unspoiled wilderness. Excellent views.
* **Tokai forest:** six charted trails, two-hour walk to Elephant's Eye cave, also called Prinseskasteel.
* **Newlands forest:** for either a ramble through the pine trees or a walk up to the saddle linking Devil's Peak with Table Mountain.

crime. The city's main thoroughfares and open spaces are safe enough in busy daylight hours and there are helpful policemen about; at other times it's wise to take your urban ramble in a group. In the countryside, stick to the recommended walking routes.

Cycling is an exhilarating way of exploring the region. The local pedal-power association organizes weekend excursions and fun rides throughout the year. The annual Cape Argus Pick 'n Pay Cycle Tour, a challenging 109km (67 miles) around the Peninsula, is held in March and accepts 35,000 entrants, partly through a ballot system. Participants must register well in advance to avoid disappointment.

Golf and **bowling** clubs welcome guests; courses and greens are of a high standard.

There are also several well-equipped and efficiently run **health studios** and clinics in the metropolitan area, some of which are part of hotels. The exclusive Hydro in Idas Valley near the attractive town of Stellenbosch caters for health-seeking visitors. A health and spa guide is available from Cape Town Tourism.

More than 300 species of birds have been identified in the wider Cape Town area, including sugarbirds, paradise flycatchers, black eagles that ride the high thermals and a variety of aquatic birds. **Bird-watchers** have a wide choice of venues. In the city centre is the Company's Garden, and in Newlands, Kirstenbosch National Botanical Gardens. To the north of the city is Milnerton lagoon and the Rietvlei Conservation Area – a major

For the Golfer

Visitors to the city are welcome at the Peninsula's many golf clubs and on the splendid courses of the Winelands to the north and east. Cape Town Tourism will provide particulars on the most popular golf courses, including Mowbray Golf Club, Rondebosch Golf Club, the Metropolitan in Mouille Point, Westlake in Lakeside, Clovelly Golf Club and the Royal Cape Golf Club in Wynberg. Driving ranges are located in Stikland, Durbanville, Maitland and at the River Club in Mowbray. Alternatively, avid golfers may contact the **Western Province Golf Union**, tel: (021) 686-1668, fax: (021) 686-1669.

waterfowl breeding reserve, home to the Caspian and Arctic tern, the fish eagle and flamingo – and a haven for contaminated or injured sea birds, particularly penguins.

Rondevlei Nature Reserve, a shallow lake surrounded by coastal dunes near the shores of False Bay, is sanctuary for an even more prolific bird life – 226 species in all. There are two lookout towers with telescopes and five hides for **bird-watching**, (the reserve also has three hippos). Another rewarding spot is the Table Mountain National Park (*see* page 59), especially the area which covers the southern tip of the Peninsula.

Organized Sport

Major provincial and international **rugby** and **cricket** matches are played at the famed Newlands stadiums, in the leafy southern suburbs 7km (4.5 miles) from the city centre. **Road running** is a popular pastime and quite competitive, the major event being the Two Oceans marathon, held over Easter each year (12,000-plus entrants). **Athletics** and **soccer** also enjoy wide support.

Apart from the spacious grounds at Newlands, sports amenities generally fall short of standards in more developed countries. Facilities in high-density townships are especially lamentable. When Cape Town was nominated to host the 2004 Olympic Games (which went to Athens), many new proposals were instituted for upgrading facilities, and government is encouraging private sponsors to continue with their plans to invest in new infrastructure for world-class sporting events, such as the 2010 Soccer World Cup.

Above: *Sea Point promenade is popular among joggers and people who walk their dogs.*
Below: *Bowling beneath the grandeur of the Table Mountain range.*

2
City and Mountain

Cape Town's most prominent thoroughfare is the old **Heerengracht**, laid out in the city's infancy. It runs straight as an arrow from the harbour, south towards the majesty of **Table Mountain**. The original route twice changed its name (the result of later decisions) – first to Adderley Street and then to Government Avenue, which passes through the exquisite **Company's Garden**. **Adderley Street** is the city's commercial heartland and the point from which, if you're on an exploratory walk-about, you should perhaps start: you'll get your bearings here, and much of what the city centre has to offer is within walking distance. **Cape Town Tourism**, the city's official source of tourism information, operates one of its Visitors' Centres in Burg Street, close to the junction with Strand Street, and stocks a comprehensive range of booklets, brochures and maps on all aspects of the city, its surrounds, its amenities and services. It also provides a **South African National Parks** reservations facility.

By African standards, this is an old city, and much from the early days remains, visible in the museums of course, but also in buildings that have survived centuries of change. Most time-honoured of these is the massive **Castle** that once guarded Cape Town against sea approaches, while among the most attractive are those erected in the later 18th century, many of them designed by the talented twosome: architect Louis Thibault and sculptor Anton Anreith. Later decades also produced their gems, notably the charmingly filigreed, wrought-iron legacies of the Victorian era that decorate **Long Street** and its neighbours.

Opposite: *The Old Town House on Greenmarket Square. Umbrellas shade the busy street-traders.*

City Centre

Malay Quarter

CITY LODGE V&A (H)

Bo-Kaap Museum

Martin Melck House (Gold of Africa Museum)

Buitengracht

New Church

Bree

Christiaan Barnard Memorial Hospital

Lutheran Church

Bree

ARABELLA SHERATON

Loop

Loop

SA Sendinggestig

HOLLOW ON THE SQUARE

Kloof St

(H) BLUE LODGE

Long

Greeenmarket Square

Long

Koopmans-De Wet House

HOLIDAY INN

Cape Town International Convention Centre

ST GEORGE'S

CAPETONIAN

Long Street Baths

Supreme Court

Old Town House

SOUTHERN SUN CAPE SUN

Heerengracht

MOUNT NELSON

Iziko South African Museum & Planetarium

Company's Garden

South African Library

ST GEORGE'S MALL

St George's Cathedral

Adderley

Fountain

Cape Town Tourism

Medipark

(H)

Bertram House

GOVERNMENT AVENUE

Tuynhuys

Groote Kerk

Golden Acre

D.F. Malan

Jewish Museum & Great Synagogue

National Art Gallery

Houses of Parliament

Iziko Slave Lodge

Railway Station

Artscape (Nico Theatre Centre)

Hatfield

St Johns

Plein

Darling

Grand Parade

Hope

City Hall

Civic Centre

AA

Magistrates' Court

Buitenkant

Gardens

Mill St

Buitenkant

Canterbury

Castle

Oswald Pirow

Buitenkant

Jutland St

Keizersgracht

Good Hope Centre

Sir Lowry

0   500 m

0   500 yd

THE FORESHORE

This flat, 145ha (358-acre) part of the northern city was reclaimed from the sea in the 1930s and 1940s. Great quantities of sand and silt were dredged up and dumped on the landward side, covering for ever the old harbour, its fine promenade and a beach that was invariably cluttered with rowing boats and oars, tackle boxes, ropes and stone anchors. Local writer Lawrence Green nostalgically recalled that, around the turn of the century, it was a memorable sight when the fishing fleet put out under spritsails, and an even more vivid one when it returned, for then 'all the old Malay priests and grey-bearded *hadjis*, all the bright-skirted womenfolk and *fezzed* small boys seemed to be waiting on the sand ...'.

The area is now bisected by the broad reaches of the **Heerengracht**, notable for its handsome flanking office blocks, its shops, and its central island of lawns, palms and fountains. There are statues of Portuguese navigator Bartolomeu Dias who rounded the Cape in 1488, founder Jan van Riebeeck and his wife Maria de la Queillerie, and, at the bottom of Adderley Street, the **War Memorial**.

If you walk east along the Hertzog Boulevard (but don't do it when the south-easter is blowing: it's little short of a wind tunnel) you'll get to the **Civic Centre** and **Artscape (Nico Theatre Centre)**, focus of Cape Town's mainstream entertainment.

At the southern end of the Heeren-gracht (or rather, its Lower Adderley Street extension) is the **railway station**, whose precincts embrace a lively flea market.

With the opening of the **Cape Town International Convention Centre** and the continual revitalization of the Central Business District and Foreshore, tourism and the conference trade are looking especially promising.

Above: *Maria, the wife of Jan van Riebeeck.*
Below: *The Heerengracht, with its sparkling fountain, is Cape Town's broadest and stateliest thoroughfare.*

Adderley Street ★

The striking feature of the city's busiest street (named after a 19th century British politician) is the vast **Golden Acre** centre, comprising a cavernous hall and con-courses packed with department stores, speciality shops and eateries. Its many glittering passageways run maze-like beneath the wider neighbourhood to link (among much else) the railway station, coach terminal, two parking garages and the sky-scraping five-star **Cape Town Holiday Inn**.

The Golden Acre is thought to be the site of the Dutch settlers' first earth-and-timber fort (the

MAN OF PEACE

Among the most powerful voices heard from the pulpit of **St George's Cathedral** was that of **Archbishop Desmond Tutu**, who headed southern Africa's Anglican community until he retired and was succeeded by Archbishop Njongonkulu Ndungane. Ordained in 1961, Tutu served as general secretary of the South African Council of Churches and Bishop of Johannesburg before accepting the archbishopric in 1986. An outspoken critic of the apartheid government and tireless campaigner for racial justice, he was awarded the **Nobel Peace Prize** in 1984 and appointed chairman of the **Truth and Reconciliation Commission** for its duration.

Below: *The cool, stone-flagged interior of Iziko Slave Lodge, part of the Cultural History Museum.*

planned site of the Castle was to be about 223m (732ft) further eastward from the fort). A small reservoir, dating back to 1663, was uncovered during building operations of the Golden Acre and a portion remains on display.

Just a few paces further up the bustling Adderley Street are the famed flower-sellers: raucous and good-humoured street vendors who invite bargain and banter and will sell you carnations, irises, roses, gladioli, and proteas – if in season – at surprisingly low prices.

The Dutch Reformed **Groote Kerk**, or 'Great Church', stands further up, on the left. It's a graceful structure, oldest of the country's formal places of worship – it was consecrated only in 1841, but incorporates the steeple and other elements of its 1704 predecessor – and is noted for its splendid pulpit, vaulted timber roofing and gravestones that serve as paving slabs. Across the street, more or less opposite, is **Edgars' City Store**, the flagship of one of the country's most popular clothing chains.

Worth at least an hour or so of sightseeing time is the **Iziko Slave Lodge Museum** at the top of Adderley Street, whose exhibits include thematic displays and a wealth of Oriental and other *objets d'art*. Rather special are the antique weapons, and the old postal stones that served as 'letter boxes' for the early Dutch trading fleets. The building started life as the slave lodge (and, less formally, as a brothel) and was later converted into the

Supreme Court. Let your eyes wander up to the rear pediment carved by Anton Anreith: it bears a caricature of the British Lion and Unicorn, rare humour from an otherwise dour Calvinistic past. Opposite, in Wale Street, is **St George's Anglican Cathedral**, where apartheid was often movingly protested. Listen to superb choral music (note the rose window) and hear the sermons of the Anglican archbishop who presides here as successor to Njongonkulu Ndungane and Nobel Laureate Desmond Tutu.

City Centre Stroll ★★

Perhaps the most pleasant of Cape Town's several piazzas is the graceful and leafy **Greenmarket Square**, where fruit and vegetable growers once marketed their wares. Most of the other open spaces have fallen victim to high-rise development and the need for inner-city parking, but Greenmarket Square has retained its earlier role to add colour and life to the central area. From Monday to Saturday the small square is crammed to its cobbled limits with umbrella-shaded street-traders' stalls heavy with bric-a-brac, craftwork, creative

Above: *The stately Houses of Parliament opposite the Company's Garden, on Government Avenue.*

clothing, leatherware, costume jewellery, fire-sale junk and, occasionally, genuine antiques. (These last are more readily available at nearby **Church Street** and **Burg Street's** paved antique mall.)

Girding Greenmarket Square are some very attractive buildings, notably the Gothic-style **Metropolitan Methodist Church** and the **Old Town House**, built in the 1750s to house the Burgher Senate (city council) and the Burgher Watch, a kind of police force cum fire-fighting squad. On view inside, beneath the star-spangled dome, are fine works of art including the Michaelis Collection, consisting of some 100 master-pieces of old Flemish and Dutch schools.

Running south to north through the city centre is **St George's Mall**, until some years ago congested with traffic but now brick-paved and reserved for pedestrians with time and a little money to spare. There are up-market shops and arcades to either side; bistros, kiosks, street stalls and buskers on the paved area.

Long Street, which runs parallel to the Mall, was the liveliest part of 19th-century Cape Town and it still

---

OPEN-AIR SHOPPING

All-purpose **street markets**, a lively feature of the city scene, are held at:
• **Greenmarket Square**
• **Grand Parade**
• **St George's Mall**
• **Railway station**
• **V&A Waterfront**
(between the Blue Shed and the Aquarium)
Antique Market:
• **Church Street**
(daily except Sundays)

Right: *The filigreed charm of Long Street. Many of the city's façades are being carefully restored.*

draws bargain-hunters, bibliophiles and serendipity shoppers with its antique and junk outlets, pawnshops and second-hand bookshops. Near the corner of Hout and Long Streets is the **Sendinggestig** – the **Missionary Meeting House Museum** and one of the city's more elegant edifices. Inside you'll see a handsome hall, galleries of yellowwood and stinkwood resting on Ionian columns, a splendid pulpit (Chinese Chippendale) and pipe organ, oak pews and teak balconies, and also displays of early missionary work at the Cape.

The upper end of the thoroughfare boasts some charming late Victorian buildings (among them the striking-looking **Blue Lodge**), many of which have received facelifts and now stand proud in their filigreed glory. While heading south towards the famous Long Street baths (heated pool, massage, Turkish steam) at the top end of the street, keep an eye open for the **Palm Tree** and **Dorp Street mosques**.

THE GARDENS AREA ★★★

Traffic thunders on all sides, but once you step into the **Company's Garden** – the area of the humble vegetable patch planted by the first Dutch settlers over three centuries ago – you're in an oasis of tranquillity.

This is one of the most beautiful of Africa's urban parks, a spacious (6ha/15-acre) expanse of manicured lawns, fountains and pools, stately trees, colourful shrubs, wandering pathways and, running along the eastern edge, oak-lined **Government Avenue**, a favourite haunt of Capetonian strollers and of cheeky little grey squirrels. Altogether, the gardens are sanctuary to more than 3000 plant species, most of them exotic. The conservatory at the mountain end contains some fine orchids and palms; close by is an aviary bustling with birds; the tea garden serves rather ordinary fare but its setting is exquisite.

Imposing edifices flank the gardens on three sides. Along the east on Government Avenue are the **Houses of Parliament**, to whose gallery the public has access (guided tours are also conducted during recess periods). The Colonial-Regency style **Tuynhuys**, once a pleasure lodge and now the president's city office, is next door. Spare a glance for the equestrian statue of General Louis Botha, guerrilla leader during the Anglo-Boer War (1899–1902) and prime minister from 1910–1919, that stands on Stal Plein in front (on the Plein Street side) of Tuynhuys.

Further up you'll find the **South African National Gallery** – repository of some 6500 works of local and European art – and another statue, a quite magnificent representation of soldier, statesman and philosopher Jan Smuts. Critics condemned it as a 'grotesque parody' when it was erected in the 1960s – and public outrage forced the commissioning of the much blander version that you'll see at the avenue's northern end in front of the **Cultural History Museum** – but it radiates power and personality. The **Great Synagogue**, an impressively domed and twin-towered Baroque building, and its neighbour, the **Old Synagogue**, were designed during the brief Egyptian Revival architectural period at the Cape, and now house the historical and ceremonial treasures of the **Jewish**

Below: *The Company's Garden began life as a vegetable patch.*

Museum. At the top of Government Avenue is **Bertram House**, an elegant Georgian period museum (early 19th-century furniture, Chinese porcelain, English silver).

African culture, the huge variety of about 200 million-year-old fossils unearthed from the strata of the Great Karoo (including dinocephalians, or 'fearful heads'), and the whales of the southern seas are prominent among the subjects displayed in the **Iziko South African Museum**, on the southwestern (Queen Victoria Street) side. Birds, fishes, geology, archaeology and the history of printing also feature. Part of the museum complex is the **Planetarium**, whose projectors reproduce the hemisphere's heavens to illuminate the constellations over a 26,000-year (past, present and future) timespan.

The garden's northern perimeter is graced by the **South African Library**, modelled on Cambridge University's Fitzwilliam Museum and a major reference institution that contains many Africana and other rare, priceless books.

The Malay Quarter ★

Along the slopes of **Signal Hill** to the west of the central area is a dense cluster of dainty little single-storey, flat-roofed houses built during the 18th century for Cape Town's cosmopolitan artisan class. The streets are narrow and steep; many of the buildings are brightly painted; the minarets of mosques rise above the low skyline, and the call of the muezzin charms the evening air.

This is the Malay Quarter, more correctly known as **Bo-Kaap**, and home to several thousand members of the Cape's Islamic society. Many of the residents are descendants of slaves who, after emancipation in the 1830s, moved into the area to form

Left: *One of the Bo-Kaap's charming mosques.*
Opposite: *The city's picturesque Malay Quarter is home to a large section of the Islamic community. Pictured is a Muslim couple, with two of the area's flat-roofed little 18th-century houses in the background.*

a very close-knit community, bound together by its Indonesian culture and faith. It remains highly integrated. The original Malay tongue is no longer spoken (Afrikaans and English are the home languages) though fragments have survived in the local songs. The community is devoutly **Muslim**.

For the rest, much of the heritage is intact, evident in the religion, in a cuisine that has evolved into a cornucopia of classic Cape dishes, in some of the customs and rituals (including the *Ratiep* sword dance, *see* panel page 18) and, on special occasions, in mode of dress.

A little of this can be seen in the **Bo-Kaap Museum** (71 Wale Street), a 1760s period house and Cape Town's oldest surviving town residence that belonged to the religious leader Abu Bakr Effendi. He hailed from Turkey and, among other things, started an Arabic school in town (he also, oddly enough, wrote one of the first books to be published in Afrikaans). The bedroom is fitted out as a traditional bridal suite; furnishings are typical of an 18th-century Muslim home.

The Bo-Kaap's **Biesmiellah** restaurant serves Malay food (no alcohol allowed). Tours can be arranged through Cape Town Tourism.

DISTRICT SIX

East of the city centre is a bare patch of ground that, until 1966, was home to 55,000 mostly **Coloured** people. In that year District Six was declared a 'white' area and officialdom began moving residents to Mitchell's Plain, 30km (19 miles) distant, and other townships on the bleak Cape Flats. The suburb was demolished – only places of worship escaped the bulldozers – in what was claimed as a slum-clearance programme. District Six had become overcrowded and unsanitary – but it also had vibrancy and a strong sense of community. The area lay fallow for three decades, an ugly scar on the cityscape and on the conscience of white society. However the land is to be returned to about 45,000 original inhabitants and their descendants. The District Six Beneficiary and Redevelopment Trust, funded by government and private donors, is monitoring the development of this important landmark.

Strand Street

This major thoroughfare once ran along the seafront (before the reclamation of the Foreshore) – the name means 'beach' – but it now cuts through the city centre, stretching down from Signal Hill to link with the motorways to the northern and southern suburbs.

It's a fairly nondescript street, but it has three points of special interest. On your left, as you come down the hill, you'll see the dignified façade of the **Lutheran Church**, built in 1771 (and later redesigned) ostensibly as a kind of warehouse – a necessary disguise since, at that time, any form of religious worship other than Dutch Reformed was barely tolerated by officialdom. The entrance, the organ loft and the splendid pulpit are the work of the sculptor and master carver Anton Anreith.

Next-door **Martin Melck House**, the original parsonage, is a fine 18th-century Cape Dutch townhouse that has been beautifully restored and now embraces the Gold Museum with a secluded garden and a charmingly serene tearoom.

The third showpiece is **Koopmans-De Wet House** (35 Strand Street), another classic example of 18th-century Cape domestic architecture. The place was home to Maria Koopmans-De Wet (1838–1906), a leading socialite, connoisseur, patron of the arts, Afrikaner nationalist and, generally, a formidable political lady who was placed under house arrest for campaigning against the infamous concentration camps of the Anglo-Boer War.

The interior re-creates the home environment of a rich and fashionable urban family during the last years of Dutch rule. On display are unusual

Above: *Koopmans-De Wet House, once home to a leading city socialite and patron of the arts.*
Left: *The old Lutheran Church on Strand Street.*

murals, an impressive collection of European and Cape (stinkwood and yellowwood) furniture, beautiful Dutch and German glassware, and some rare porcelain.

THE CASTLE AREA ★★★

The massive, five-sided, stone-walled fort, completed in 1679, was originally designed to guard the fledgling Dutch colony from sea invasion but later served as the military, administrative and social hub of the colony.

The **Castle** has an imposing entrance, embellished with a clock tower, the crest of the United Netherlands, the Dutch East India Company's monogram ('VOC') and the coats of arms of the Company's six chambers in Holland. The tower's bell, cast in 1697, is still rung on occasion. Bisecting the spacious courtyard is a defensive cross-wall known as 'De Kat', which once supported cannon but later became notable for a gracefully balustraded rococo balcony (Klein Kat) that looks down on the one-time governor's residence and the grand reception hall.

Much of the Castle is open to the public. On display in the Governor's residence are period furnishings, *objets d'art*, ceramics and paintings of the celebrated William Fehr collection.

The original moat and wooden bridge have been restored; other recent renovations and additions include a military museum, the historic Dolphin Pool, a period house (the Secunde's quarters), two **dungeons**

Below: *Much of the Castle, including its historic moat, has been carefully restored.*

and the Granary that contains artefacts unearthed during restoration work (old Dutch clay pipes, pieces of porcelain, and there is a transverse section of the Castle's original foundation).

There's a very pleasant restaurant, De Goewerneur – which specializes in traditional Cape cuisine – in the courtyard. The 'ceremony of the keys' takes place at 10:00 and 12:00 on weekdays, and Saturdays during holidays, or on request. The Castle also offers guided tours at 11:00, 12:00 and 14:00 Monday to Saturday, as well as self-guided walkabouts where visitors follow a route mapped out in seven languages.

Outside the walls, on the western side, is the **Grand Parade**, where colonial troops mustered in their uniformed glory. It is now a 'pay and display' parking area and a not-very-stylish open-air market. It is also where crowds periodically gather in protest or in celebration – here, for instance, Nelson Mandela spoke conciliatory words to a quarter-million throng hours after his release from prison in 1990. Mandela delivered his address from the balcony of the flanking **City Hall**, a grandly ornate granite and marble edifice designed in the Italian Renaissance style and completed in 1905. Its clock tower, modelled on, though just half the size of that of London's Big Ben, houses southern Africa's largest carillon of 39 bells.

Above: *The entrance to the Castle. Completed in 1679, it is the country's oldest occupied building.*
Right: *The turn-of-the-century City Hall, built of ornate granite in the Italian Renaissance style.*

The main hall, where orchestral concerts are often held, has a 3165-pipe organ and is venue for the more lavish of civic functions.

TABLE MOUNTAIN ★★★

South Africa's best-known physical feature dominates the Peninsula's northern skyline. The great flat-topped sandstone massif towers 1087m (3566ft) above the city and measures nearly 3km (2 miles) from end to end, and on a sunny day its distinctive shape can be discerned from 200km (124 miles) out to sea. From the summit there are spectacular views of Cape Town, its harbour and the Waterfront below, of **Devil's Peak** and **Lion's Head** to either side, of the hazy and majestic Hottentots Holland mountains in the east and Cape Point far to the south.

The heights, though, are often obscured by what's known as the 'tablecloth': dense clouds that billow across its rim to tumble down the northern precipice in a continuous cascade. The phenomenon is the product of the southeasterly sea-wind ('Cape Doctor'), which can reach speeds of around 100kph (62mph). It sweeps moisture from False Bay against the massive rampart, causing the droplets to rise, cool and condense into a thick cover. At these times the Table Mountain Aerial Cableway is not accessible to visitors.

TABLE MOUNTAIN ODDITIES

• The mountain sustains more **plant species** than the whole of the British Isles.
• It supports some uniquely adapted forms of wildlife, including dassies, **rock rabbits** (hyraxes) which have evolved sticky feet for a better grip on the steep slopes.
• One of the inhabitants of the mountain's caves is a pale, blind species of the **peripatus**, the 'missing link' between insects and worms.
• Among many hermits of the mountain was **Joshua Penny**, a runaway American sailor who hid on the slopes for 14 months in the early 1800s. He later (in 1815) said he had 'never enjoyed life better than when I lived among the ferocious animals of Table Mountain, because I had secured myself against the more savage English'.

Left: *Cape Town panorama, with Table Mountain rising 1087m (3566ft) above the city.*

Above, opposite: *Table Mountain – the view from the top, the cable car and the upper cable station.*

The ancient **Khoisan** knew the massif as 'Hoeri Kwaggo' – Mountain of the Sea – but it has had many names. The one that endured was bestowed by the first European to climb to the top: **Antônio de Saldanha**, an adventurous Portuguese admiral who made the ascent in 1503 (he was later to be killed in a skirmish with the west-coast Hottentots).

Saldanha had to beat a way to the top; today five strenuous but straightforward and excellent walking paths lead to the summit, and there are many more suitable only for more experienced hikers and climbers.

Those who make their way up the slopes – through the woodlands of the heavily watered slopes and Back Table – can spot almost half of the 2600-odd plants indigenous to the Cape Peninsula.

The Cableway ★★★

Most visitors ride up in the modern gondolas which replaced the old cable cars when the Table Mountain Aerial Cableway Company upgraded its facilities in 1997. The Swiss-manufactured cars, boasting revolving floors and a magnificent 360-degree view over the city and beyond, carry up to 65 individuals at a time. The comfortable six-minute trip may be taken at virtually any time of the year – from 08:00–22:00 in summer and 08:30–18:00 in winter. The service is, however, suspended if the wind exceeds 80kph (48mph) although this is not very common even in windy Cape Town. Fortunately the carrying capacity of the R7-million cars has largely eliminated the seemingly endless queues which plagued the old service and, as a result, prior reservations are no longer taken. The wait is thus short and the rewards breathtaking. Along with

the renovation of the cableway system, facilities at both the foot and the top of the mountain have been upgraded, with a smart new restaurant and souvenir outlet at the top and restaurant facilities near the lower station.

To get to the lower terminus, drive up Kloof Nek, take the Kloof Nek bus from Adderley Street or be adventurous and call a Rikki taxi (tel: 0861 745 547). A shuttle operates between Kloof Nek and the lower station in peak season (you could walk this but it's a fair way).

Climbing Up

The more energetic visitor may prefer to make the ascent on foot. Some of the established paths are gentle enough (it is a two-hour uphill walk from the back, or southern slopes, of the mountain), others are more strenuous, and some are downright dangerous.

All the routes should be treated with respect. It is easy to get lost, which can be a frightening experience if the weather turns nasty – as it can do, suddenly and

Above: *A pair of dassies. Here, they have evolved 'sticky' feet for a better grip on the steep slopes.*
Below: *At the top of Table Mountain, looking south across the expanse of False Bay to Cape Point.*

without any warning at all. Invest in a good map and guidebook (available in city bookshops); choose a route that is well within your physical capability; do not stray from the path; and, if it's your first trip, arrange to make it in the company of someone who knows the terrain. Leave word of your route and estimated time of return with a friend. Wear warm clothing and stout walking shoes.

These are elementary precautions, but a surprising number of **climbers** ignore them – and the mountain regularly takes its toll on human life.

On the Summit

Each year hundreds of thousands of people take the cableway to the summit. At the top there is a **restaurant** and a **souvenir shop** – from where you can send a fax, or mail a letter bearing the Table Mountain postmark. Along the tabletop are some superb observation points. Wall plaques describe the mountain's nature reserve and the plants that grace the slopes during the different seasons. The walk to **Maclear's Beacon**, the mountain's highest point, takes about 50 minutes. The best time to make the summertime ascent is probably in the early evening (around 18:00), when you can watch the sun set and the colours change over the sea and land. Then stay on for a pleasant dinner at the restaurant and watch the lights come on in the city and harbour.

The Flanking Peaks ★

Also worth exploring are the imposing formations that stand to either side of Table Mountain. To the west you'll see the sugarloaf shape of **Lion's Head** and its attendant ridge, which ends in the 'rump' of **Signal Hill**, the whole vaguely resembling a lion *couchant*.

You can climb to the top of the 669m (2195ft) **Lion's Head** peak; chains and ladders help on the most challenging stretches. There are dramatic views from the crest. It is something of a tradition to climb Lion's Head to watch the full moon rise but the occasion brings hoards of people to the peak so getting down can take hours.

A lot less arduous is the drive up **Signal Hill**, from where the vistas are as rewarding. Each day the noon gun is fired from its emplacement on the hill – a sound which tells Capetonians of their impending lunch break, though its real purpose is to remind listeners of those who fought and died in World War I and II. The hill's name derives not from the gun, but from an earlier semaphore station that used to communicate with ships at sea. The area is a favourite spot for picnics.

The drive up will take you past four of the Peninsula's six *kramats* – sacred tombs of Muslim holy men who are believed to extend their protective power over the city.

Devil's Peak, on the left as you look up from the city, is notable for three British blockhouses built on its steep slopes 'to maintain a very fine command of the Bay'. The ascent to the summit, about 1000m (3281ft) above sea level, is only for experienced hikers and climbers.

Above: *One of the steep hiking trails in the mountain's deep ravines.*

THE EASTERN BUTTRESS

Devil's Peak, the high buttress that guards Table Mountain's eastern flank, was once an important part of Cape Town's defence. After British troops invaded and occupied the Peninsula in 1795, their commander General, Sir James Craig, built **three blockhouses** on the higher slopes. They were named **King's, Queen's** and the **Duke of York's**. King's later served as a convict station, and is now a historical monument. The peak itself is 1002m (3288ft) high and can be reached only by fit and experienced hikers and climbers.

3 The Atlantic Seaboard and Northern Suburbs

For two centuries early Cape Town developed around and relied heavily on its harbour, but it wasn't until after the middle of the 19th century that its single jetty was replaced by sturdier installations. In 1860 Prince Alfred tipped the first wagonload of stone for the new Alfred Basin (the Victoria Basin and the twin signal towers were built in 1883).

Later development reclaimed the present **Foreshore** area from the sea, creating the huge Duncan Dock. Later still came the 366m (1200ft) Sturrock dry dock, one of the largest in the world; the Robinson graving dock; the Ben Schoeman container terminal; and the enormous pre-cooling stores that handle the Western Cape's bountiful export fruit harvests.

Table Bay harbour also embraces the **Royal Cape Yacht Club**. The rather exclusive club hosts a number of sleek, handsome, high-tech craft, and their crews, at its clubhouse and marina on Duncan Dock. After a long absence, a growing number of large, glamorous cruise ships are also docking.

The older part of the area, the Victoria and Alfred basins, also draws the interest: they have been transformed into a brilliantly animated tourist playground that rivals Table Mountain as the region's premier tourist attraction.

The Peninsula's 'Atlantic' coastline runs from Table Bay south for 54km (34 miles) to the edge of the Table Mountain National Park – a route that unveils land- and seascapes breathtaking in their splendour.

THE OCEAN RACERS

Cape Town harbour features as a major station on some of the world's most prestigious yachting routes, including the **South Atlantic Race (formerly known as the Cape-to-Rio)**, the **Volvo Ocean Race**, and the **BT** single-handed round-the-world races. The premier local round-the-buoys event is **Royal Cape Yacht Club/ Table Bay International Sailing Week**, which takes place in December.

Opposite: The broad sweep of Camps Bay.

PRISON HOTEL

The Waterfront's **Breakwater Lodge** and **MBA campus** is a complex with a difference: it's part of the original, old **Breakwater Prison**, built in 1859 (and later extended) to house long-term convicts assigned to work on Table Bay's dock construction programme. The prison's original façade and court-yard have been retained, but the rest of the complex was rebuilt to create the modern, 300-bedroom lodge as well as premises for the University of Cape Town's **Graduate School of Business**. The school's facilities include seven lecture theatres, 50 seminar rooms, a high-tech library, restaurant, cafeteria and bar. On view is a tread-mill, installed in 1890 to keep the prisoners in order.

Below: *One of the many Cape fur seals that bask at the quayside.*

THE WATERFRONT ★★★

Not too long ago **Table Bay** and its docklands were very much part of Capetonian daily life, but with land reclamation (the Foreshore) and highway construction the links were severed. Gone was the seafront leisure beach and the small fishing boats (*see page 28*), to be replaced by oil storage tanks, a wilderness of grimy buildings and barriers, and a raised motorway that stands as a monument to poor planning and bad taste.

Now sea and city have merged again, reunited by the **Victoria & Alfred Waterfront** scheme, a multibillion rand venture that has revitalized the docks. It draws its inspiration from successful harbour projects in San Francisco, Sydney and elsewhere, but it is not simply a copy: it is designed to meet local needs; it has its own distinctive personality, and its setting, beneath the moody grandeur of Table Mountain, is both unique and

Places of Interest
1. Time Ball Tower
2. Old Port Captain's Building
3. Waterfront Clocktower Precinct
4. Vaughn Johnson's Wine Shop
5. Mitchell's Brewery and Ferryman's
6. Telkom Exploratorium
7. King's Warehouse
8. Red Shed Craft Workshop
9. Waterfront Trading Company
10. The Pierhead
11. Quay 4
12. SA Maritime Museum
14. BMW Pavilion
15. Agfa Amphitheatre
16. NSRI

Victoria and Alfred Waterfront

exciting. Nor is it just a pleasure ground. The V&A is still very much a working area; the graving docks, originally built for the tall ships of yesteryear, continue to function; salt-stained fishing craft use the basins; tugs and tour boats move up and down; offices and apartments are being built and new developments are in progress.

For the most part, though, the open quaysides are for tourists and the leisure-bent locals. The scheme is by no means complete, but the more interesting and colourful of the existing structures have already been converted, and a lot of new ones built, to serve as restaurants, hotels, umbrella-shaded bistros, bars, coffee shops, cinemas, museums, markets (craft, fish, produce), speciality stores, entertainment centres and the world-class **Two Oceans Aquarium** (see panel, page 48). Other attractions in progress, or planned, include a small-craft marina, a promenade, public squares, walkways, a steam railway station and a waterway leading all the way into the city centre.

Above: *The Two Oceans Aquarium.*

Sights to See

The Waterfront is for relaxation – for eating, drinking, shopping, and for soaking up the charming atmosphere – rather than for sightseeing. But a fair amount that is of historical interest will emerge as you stroll the precincts.

Take note of the **Time Ball Tower**, once used by passing ships to set their clocks, and the **Old Port Captain's building** (the Waterfront's headquarters). Across the Cut, on the opposite side is the **Old Clock Tower** (which housed the clock mechanism on the topmost floor and, on the bottom floor, the tide-gauge, operated by a float on the water below). Cape fur seals, oblivious of the passing parade, sun themselves around Victoria Basin.

There is a well-stocked **Wine Centre** next door to the visitor information office, and further along is the small **Mitchell's Brewery** that produces superb draught ale.

Shopping

Principal shopping centre is the huge **Victoria Wharf** Shopping Centre: a complex of converted warehouses crammed with up-market outlets ranging from a biltong bar (biltong is dried raw meat, and a prized South African delicacy) through jewellery, clothing and accessories boutiques, to some of the country's most imaginative craft shops.

THE SEA ON SHOW

The walk-through, window-lined tunnels of the V&A Waterfront's **Two Oceans Aquarium** give you a scuba diver's view of the Cape coast's undersea wonders. Here, in all their colourful variety, are sharks, tuna and about 300 other species that together form a representative cross section of the region's marine heritage. Highlights include above- and below-water observation of seals and penguins; a 'touch tide pool' containing starfish, sea urchins and much else; a kelp forest, open ocean tank and special displays of rays and jellyfish. Fascinating attractions include a complete coastal ecosystem in miniature, with waterfalls, mountain streams, mud banks, sand flats and inter-tidal rock pools, all stocked with appropriate plant, bird and marine life.

The Wharf is open until late, seven days a week. Next door, the **King's Warehouse** houses a cornucopia of produce and fine food stores.

Make a point, too, of visiting the **Red Shed Craft Workshop** (ceramics, jewellery, textiles, basketware, township art, candles) and African Heritage (beadwork, woven goods and much else). There's also the **Waterfront Trading Company**, where you'll find an enormous selection of local handwork.

Other shopping clusters are located at the **Clock Tower Precinct**, the **Victoria and Alfred Hotel** (the Alfred Mall) and at the historic **Pierhead**.

Food, Drink and Entertainment

There are restaurants for all pockets and preferences; the menus on offer range from traditional Cape fare and seafood, through Mediterranean, Cajun, Italian, Chinese and Mexican to *haute cuisine*. Several of the eateries are also taverns (**Ferryman's** and **Quay Four** are among the most popular) that occasionally feature live music and entertainment. The **Sports Café** pub and restaurant combines conviviality with sporting interest: television sets beam local and international events while patrons watch, eat, drink and make merry.

A fast-food mall offers a wide variety of 'food to go'

while a number of coffee bars and bistros cater for those with more sophisticated tastes. There are also a number of speciality stores such as one specializing in sweets, another in wine and there's even one dedicated to selling a wide range of mineral water.

For people of all ages the Waterfront is in fact an Aladdin's Cave of delights. Open-air entertainment (including concerts and buskers), a variety of festivals, a gem-

Left: *The imaginatively conceived Waterfront area.*
Opposite: *An outdoor concert draws the crowds.*
Below: *Victoria Wharf shopping mall.*

stone scratch patch, and boat and helicopter trips are among the drawcards. A monthly events calendar, *Good Times*, is available from the information kiosk.

Getting Around

For gentle sightseeing, there's the Waterfront historical walk (details from the Waterfront information centre) and round-the-harbour boat trips. If you're feeling more adventurous, and want a bird's-eye view of the wider scene, take a helicopter flip around the harbour, city bowl or further afield. Sea cruises (to Robben Island, among other destinations), game-fishing excursions and boat charters are also available. A regular bus service operates between the city centre and Waterfront. There's ample parking for private cars or you can take a water taxi from the Arabella Sheraton.

ROBBEN ISLAND ★★

About 11.5km (7 miles) north out to sea and clearly visible from the shore is oval-shaped Robben Island ('robben' is Dutch for 'seals'), which until recently served as the infamous maximum security prison where **Nelson**

TRIPS AND TOURS BY AIR

For a memorable bird's-eye view of the city and surrounding areas, book a helicopter flip. Companies offer excursions ranging from a ten-minute jaunt around the city bowl and Table Mountain to an hour's flight south along the scenically stunning Atlantic seaboard to Cape Point and back over False Bay. Various tours take you further afield – to the picturesque Winelands, for instance, where you spend time sightseeing, sampling the vintages and lunching at one of the stately homesteads. Among aerial tour operators are: Civair, NAC Sport Helicopters, The Hopper and Executive Helicopters (see page 121). Destinations include Hermanus, the Garden Route, Langebaan Lagoon and, in springtime, flower-bedecked Namaqualand.

Mandela, South Africa's first truly democratically elected president, served much of his 27-year sentence.

Today, Robben Island has a new and far more amiable image. Since the early 1990s government and concerned groups have been transforming it into a national treasure, to the point where, in 1999, it gained status as a **World Heritage Site**. Conservationists are preserving the island as a forest reserve, and as a breeding ground for birds such as Caspian and Damara terns and rare African, or jackass, penguins. There are now about 132 bird species on the island. These and its other assets – the wild flowers (arum lilies are everywhere), the rugged coastline, and above all Robben Island's prominence in the story of the liberation struggle – place it in the top ranks of visitor attractions.

The 574ha (1418-acre) island's history goes back a long way. Early Portuguese, Dutch and English mariners on their way to and from the Orient visited its shores for fresh provisions (seals, penguins and birds' eggs), and on two occasions in the early 1600s it was used to confine convicts. Later, the first Dutch colonists collected its seashells (to produce lime), and its 'beautifully veined' slate and dressed stone to construct the Castle and some of infant Cape Town's other buildings.

Over the decades Robben Island also served variously as a giant livestock pen, a place for lunatics and

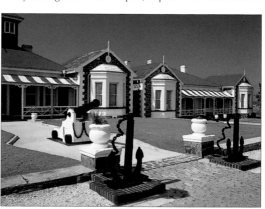

Right: *Robben Island's Old Residency, once the commissioner's home.*

paupers, the chronically sick and the otherwise unwanted (their suffering caused a public outcry that eventually put an end to the abuses), a leper colony – and then as a penal colony.

At one stage, the inmates included political prisoners, among them some high-born exiles from Holland's Eastern possessions such as the Princes of Ternate and Madura. They are commemorated in the island's *kramat*. Another prominent prisoner was the Xhosa prophet Makhanda, who led his people in a 'holy war' against the colonists. He was consigned to Robben Island in 1819, organized a mass escape and drowned when the boat capsized in a storm.

This living museum supports a tiny village of about 1200 inhabitants. Among notable structures are the 1800s lighthouse, which still performs with honour; the **Church of the Good Shepherd**, designed by celebrated turn-of-the-century architect Herbert Baker, and the **Old Residency**, once the home of the local commissioners.

Other features date from World War II, when the island played a role in Cape Town's sea defences. The major focal point is the **Maximum Security Prison**, a bleak place of tiny cells (including Mandela's). The island bus tour also takes in **Robert Sobukwe's prison house**, the lime quarry where the prisoners worked, and other historic venues.

Only the **Robben Island Museum** conducts official tours of the island and bookings may be made through the Nelson Mandela Gateway to Robben Island at the Clock Tower Precinct, V&A Waterfront. The 3½-hour island tour includes a return boat trip, a visit to the prison, interaction with ex-political prisoners and a bus tour (*see* page 121 for contact details).

Above: *Bird's-eye view of Robben Island, used over the centuries to confine political prisoners and other 'undesirables'.*

ROBBEN ISLAND MUSEUM

The Robben Island Museum (RIM) manages a fine collection of artefacts, documents, photographs, art works and audiovisual material housed in the University of the Western Cape Robben Island Mayibuye Archives, the museum's official collections unit. The Archives provide a unique record of South African history and culture, particularly with regard to the apartheid period, the freedom struggle and political imprisonment.

MAN OF DESTINY

Nelson Mandela, president from 1994 to 1999, was incarcerated for treason on Robben Island.

Born in 1918 into the royal Tembu (Xhosa) house in the Transkei region of the Eastern Cape, Mandela qualified as a lawyer during the 1940s and quickly became prominent in the movement to liberate the country from apartheid, helping to found *Umkhonto we Sizwe*, the military wing of the **African National Congress**, in the 1950s. Finally indicted for conspiring to commit nearly 200 acts of sabotage, he was convicted at the famed Rivonia trial of 1963 and sentenced to life imprisonment. On his release in 1990 he chose the path of peace, employing his skills and immense moral stature to lead South Africa to freedom and democracy.

THE RIVIERA

The coastal road that leads southwest from **Table Bay** traverses an 8km (5-mile) shoreline of rocky indentations, entrancing expanses of white sand and charming little coves around which cluster some of the city's most fashionable residential areas.

Thereafter, the maritime highway – **Victoria Drive** – takes you along the coast through scenically stunning landscapes to **Hout Bay**. Continue via the recently upgraded **Chapman's Peak** toll road along the cliff side and round to **Scarborough** before turning inland to the **Table Mountain National Park.**

To drive along this route, at any time of the day, but especially at the magical sunset hour, is delight indeed. On your left, for much of the way, are the often cloud-wreathed heights of the **Twelve Apostles**, part of the Table Mountain range. On your right are jagged cliffs that tumble down to rocks and the blue ocean.

The Seaside Suburbs ★

West of the city is **Green Point**, site of the new sports stadium to host the 2010 Soccer World Cup. The Mouille Point Lighthouse is the oldest in the country: its giant oil lantern first shone in 1824, later to be replaced by an 850,000-candlepower lamp that can be seen 23km

(14 miles) out to sea. The local hospital, New Somerset (actually over 100 years old), houses the Cape Medical Museum, worth a visit for its fascinating relics of modern medicine's pioneering days. Of special interest is the re-created Victorian dentist's surgery. Also note the photograph of the somewhat effeminate Dr James Barry, who performed the country's first Caesarean section and went on to become inspector-general of

Britain's army hospitals. On his death, so the story goes, it was revealed that Barry was a woman, though the story was never conclusively substantiated.

Next-door **Sea Point** is a busy, bustling, cosmopolitan area dense with luxurious apartment and time-share blocks, hotels, restaurants, discos, delis and nightspots. The Main Road is a glitzy, noisy, fun thoroughfare, though the tinsel is a bit tarnished in places (it has lost much of its custom to the harbour Waterfront). The long (3km; 2-mile) lawn- and palm-graced promenade is much favoured by Capetonian strollers. At the end of Beach Road is the Sea Point Pavilion. The main feature is the large sea-water swimming pool.

Above: *Clifton's beaches in high summer. The water tends to be chilly, but the sands are sheltered from the prevailing wind.*
Opposite: *Sea Point, a cosmopolitan place of smart beachfront apartments, a myriad eateries and a stunning promenade.*

From Sea Point you drive through **Bantry Bay** to **Clifton**, famed for its four inviting beaches, each divided from its neighbour by a jumble of granite boulders, and sheltered from the southeasterly wind. Third Beach is popular among the trendy young while Fourth Beach is usually packed with families. Note that parking is a problem; only Fourth has vehicular access. There aren't many visitor facilities – the suburb has managed to resist commercial inroads, retaining its quiet dignity at the expense of tourism infrastructure.

The hillside slopes support the houses of the rich (and occasionally famous); beyond, towering high above suburb and sea, are the backing massifs: **Lion's Head** and the first of the Apostles that form the western coastal rampart. They are infinitely changeable in their mood, and breathtaking in their grandeur. Hugging the sheer cliffside below the road are massed banks of luxury apartments and houses.

Right: *A scenic view of the Hout Bay harbour with its fishing trawlers.*

Atlantic Seaboard

Camps Bay, further along, also boasts a fine expanse of sand, but has more amenities (tidal pool, shops, theatre, restaurants, and an excellent hotel called The Bay), though both centres remain affluent residential areas rather than playgrounds.

HOUT BAY ★★★

After a twisting and visually spectacular 15km (9-mile) drive along the coast road you'll see, nestled among the rocks far below on your right, the picture-postcard village of **Llandudno**. It rests in a precipitous valley beneath a peak known as Little Lion's Head, and boasts a lovely, secluded beach (the flanking **Sunset Rocks** invite quiet contemplation at twilight) and its own shipwreck.

Walk for about 20 minutes down the shoreline and you'll get to **Sandy Bay**, prime venue for those in search of an all-over tan. Much larger than Llandudno but equally attractive is adjacent **Hout Bay**, a fishing harbour and rapidly growing residential town girded by magnificent mountain slopes. 'Hout' is the Afrikaans word for 'wood': the name derived from the area's value as a source of timber in the early colonial days. But the hillsides are still reassuringly tree-mantled.

Hout Bay's picturesque small harbour is the head-quarters of the Peninsula's crayfish (rock lobster) fleet; other catches include tasty snoek, which is sold on the quay from June until August. The annual **Snoek Festival** occupies a lively weekend during this period. Busy throughout the year is **Mariner's Wharf**, a complex modelled on its namesake in San Francisco and embracing seafood bistro, restaurant, fresh fish and live lobster market (also on sale are closed oysters; any pearls you find are yours to keep), nautical gift and curio shops. Battered working boats and squeaky clean leisure craft rub shoulders along the moorings. Just a short way beyond is the ever-popular fish-and-chips takeaway, **Fish on the Rocks**.

Several boat companies takes sightseers on sunset 'champagne' **cruises** to Cape Town's Waterfront, 20km (12 miles) distant, and on shorter trips to nearby **Duiker Island**, where in summertime a myriad sea birds – most of them fairly rare Bank cormorants – and more than 6000 Cape fur seals bask on the rocky shores. Seals are common inhabitants of the Peninsula and west coast, remarkably comfortable in the presence of people and so numerous that commercial fishermen claim they make serious inroads into marine resources. The culling of seals – both to control their numbers and for their meat, blubber and pelts – has provoked fierce controversy.

Charter companies advertise deep-sea **game-fishing** (contact Cape Town Tourism for details), and other attractions include the **Hout Bay Museum** (information on guided walks available) and the **World of Birds**.

The annual Red Bull Big Wave Surfing competition takes place, weather conditions permitting, every year off Dungeons, a reef just outside Hout Bay Harbour. It can only take place once the surf is in excess of four metres!

CHAPMAN'S PEAK AND BEYOND **

Southward still, the coast road has in the past suffered grievous rock falls, but thanks to recent major repairs, Chapman's Peak Drive has regained

> **SANDY BAY**
>
> Until recently this was South Africa's only nude beach although not officially recognized as such. It tends to be a bit crowded, but there's more to the place than nubile nudity: the steeply rising hinterland is covered by the Cape's unique *fynbos* vegetation, and there's pleasant seclusion to be found among the beachfront boulders.

Below: *Viewing peaceful Hout Bay from Chapman's Peak Drive. The imposing massif at the left is known as The Sentinel.*

its place as one of the region's finest scenic routes. Winding precariously along the mountain for about 10km (6 miles) from Hout Bay to Noordhoek, the heart-stopping toll road twists its way 600m (1970ft) to the highest point to reveal views of memorable splendour, including the view northwards towards **Hout Bay** with its distinctive **Sentinel buttress** and the distant green hills of **Constantia**.

As Chapman's Peak Drive ends, you come into the lagoon-laced **Noordhoek** flatlands, fringed by **Long Beach**. Noordhoek is still rural – charmingly so – and the haunt of an unusual number of artists and crafts-persons. Horse Trail Safaris and Dunes stables organize beach rides; contact Cape Town Tourism for details.

From here you can either head across the waist of the Peninsula to the **False Bay** town of **Fish Hoek** or take the M65 south to **Kommetjie**, a delightful little seaside centre that offers good angling, surfing, bird-watching and (rather chilly) bathing. After Kommetjie is **Scarborough** – a cluster of holiday houses set in a wilderness of heath.

THE NORTHERN SUBURBS

The area to the north and east of central Cape Town has tended, undeservedly, to remain outside the tourism mainstream over the years, but that has all changed with the development of a number of splendid new (and some not-so-new) venues for the shopper, the gambler and the leisure-bent visitor.

Tyger Valley shopping centre is one of Cape Town's best. The centre boasts nearly 300 speciality and general retail outlets, approximately 40 restaurants and eateries, and 10 cinemas. Also drawing the shopper is the equally impressive N1 City complex and the Sanlam Centre.

The Mayibuye centre at the university of the Western Cape is well worth visiting. It has a huge and fascinating collection of documents and photos relating to the liberation struggle, and other hitherto unnoticed material from South Africa's past.

Durbanville, an attractively green residential area 30km (19 miles) north of the city centre, is noted for its racecourse, its lovely rose garden (thousands of plants on show; cream teas served) and its nature reserve, where you can picnic and watch the busy bird life. Durbanville also has its own wine route, which leads you to half a dozen cellars that produce fine vintages.

Rietvlei is located in Milnerton, not far from central Cape Town. This wetland reserve ranks as one of the Western Cape's premier bird sanctuaries.

Century City, also in Milnerton, is a shopper's dream that is growing rapidly to embrace a convention centre, hotel, waterfront, canals, Intaka Island, its small-craft harbour and environmentally important wetlands. Newest and most prominent elements are its Canal Walk shopping complex (largest in the southern hemisphere) and the beguiling MTN ScienCentre. A corporate park and large residential component (3700 units) are being developed. Century has been referred to as the country's first 'intelligent city', featuring advanced IT systems and a sophisticated range of e-business services for its retail, corporate and residential occupants.

GrandWest Casino and Entertainment World, on Vanguard Drive in Goodwood, opened in December 2000 – the city's inaugural gambling mecca. It embraces 66 gaming tables and 1750 slots – and much else besides, including two hotels, restaurants, nightspots, watering holes, ice rink (Olympic size), six cinemas, and a children's theme park.

Below: *The vibrant GrandWest casino and entertainment world.*

The **Cape Town Ostrich Ranch**, home to a fine community of these big birds, offers tours, a gift shop and restaurant (which, of course, serves ostrich dishes).

The ranch is off the N7 highway 30km (19 miles) from central Cape Town.

4
The Eastern Seaboard

The Peninsula's eastern coastline, from **Cape Point** to **Cape Hangklip**, is lapped by the warm and often wind-tossed waters of **False Bay,** one of coastal South Africa's foremost holiday playgrounds.

False Bay's rather odd name derives from the less benevolent side of its nature. Many an early seafarer mistook the Point for Hangklip and thought they were in Table Bay – a serious navigational error – and over the centuries ships were regularly driven ashore by the perverse winds and currents. The sea here still, occasionally, takes its toll of traffic, but for the most part the shores are kindly, a mecca for the bather and boating enthusiast, the fisherman and the underwater explorer.

TABLE MOUNTAIN NATIONAL PARK

Almost 8000ha (19,770 acres) of the Peninsula's southern section is occupied by Table Mountain National Park, a rather bleak but plant-rich expanse of fynbos (heather) vegetation that, come springtime, is magically transformed by multicoloured swathes of wild flowers. The reserve has few trees – just a scatter of wind-bent milkwoods manage to withstand the fierce south-easterly winds – but more than 1200 flowering species have been identified within its bounds, and more, as yet unlogged, await the inquisitive botanist. It also sustains wildlife: **Cape mountain zebra**, **Cape fox, caracal** and a variety of **antelope**, including the once threatened but now flourishing **bontebok**. The area is also home to about five troops of **chacma baboons**.

BEWARE THE BABOONS

The chacma baboons of **Table Mountain National Park** are thought to be the only primates in the world (apart from fish-eating man) that live largely off the fruits of the sea, which they garner from the rock pools and beaches at low tide.
The baboons are partial to human handouts but in your own interest, and in theirs, keep your vehicle locked and *do not feed them.*

Opposite: *Villages gird the shores of False Bay.*

Above: *Looking down from Cape Point.*
Opposite: *The Vasco da Gama monument.*

EXPLORING ON FOOT

Visitors are free to walk where they wish in Table Mountain National Park, though seven routes have been charted and signposted. These range from the one-hour Kanonkop Trail on the eastern side to the four-hour (one-way) Good Hope Coastal Walk that takes you from Cape Point along the western shoreline from near Cape Point to the wreck site of the good ship *Phyllisia*. There is also an excellent two-day trail around the reserve with very well appointed overnight huts near Cape Point. A map of the trail network is available at the reserve's entrance, and the information centre has details of the ongoing programme of walks and trails. About 20km (12 miles) of tar and gravel roads are also open to mountain bikers; for information, contact Day-trippers, tel: (021) 511-4766.

Over 160 different kinds of **avifauna** have been recorded within the reserve, including the tiny **sunbird**, the **black eagle** and such ocean-going species as **albatross**, and **cormorant**.

The terrain, broken by a ridge of hills running down the False Bay side, is cut through by a network of roads, trails and paths that lead to picnic and barbecue sites, beaches, coves and viewing points.

Despite some concern for the ecology of the region, facilities for the almost half a million annual visitors have been upgraded to include the Two Oceans Restaurant, one of the Peninsula's favourite dining experiences, and a funicular to ferry visitors to the exceptional viewing spots. Other amenities include an information centre, a souvenir shop, a small slipway, tidal pools and superb scuba-diving and snorkelling spots. On calm days, underwater visibility is good, and the marine life both colourful and fascinating.

Cape Point ★★★

The reserve's chief drawcard is unquestionably the massive and spectacular headland at the tip of the Peninsula. Cape Point's cliffs fall sheer for about 300m (985ft) to the ocean, in whose often turbulent waters you can glimpse shoals of **tuna** and **snoek**, sporting **dolphins** and **seals** and, occasionally, the massive bulk of a **southern right whale**. Birds are quite plentiful too – **albatross**, **petrel**, **gannet** and **gull** wheel and cry in the air around the promontory.

- The *Joanna* (near Quoin Point; 1682). The first recorded British wreck, the vessel sank with 70 chests of treasure. Salvagers recovered 300kg (660lb) of bullion and 25,000 coins in 1982.
- The *Dageraad* (Robben Island; 1694). Sank with 17 chests of silver pieces that had been salvaged from an earlier wreck. Only nine chests were recovered.
- The *Birkenhead* (Danger Point; 1852). The 600 British troops (most of whom were drowned) stood to attention as passengers were rescued, hence the heroic phrase 'Women and children first'.
- The tankers *Romelia* and *Antipolis* (Llandudno and Oudekraal, 1977).

Breathtaking vistas untold from the base of the old (1857) lighthouse at the top: from here your eye takes in the far ocean horizons and the sweep of **False Bay** to **Danger Point**, 80km (50 miles) to the east.

Cape Point has its place in seafaring myth. It is off this headland that the *Flying Dutchman*, a phantom sailing ship with tattered sails and storm-swept decks, has periodically been sighted. Legend has it that a 17th-century Dutch captain, Hendrik van der Decken, his craft crippled by the southern gales, vowed to round the 'Cape of Storms' even if it took him until the Day of Judgement to achieve. Best-known of the many sightings was that recorded in 1880 by a Royal Navy officer, a young midshipman who, in 1907, became Britain's King George V.

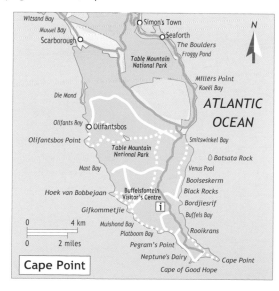

Cape Point

Below: *Simon's Town's main street, known as the Historical Mile.*

FALSE BAY

From Cape Point northwards, the bay is fringed by a 30km (19-mile), almost continuous, stretch of beach. A number of old, established and attractive seaside centres are also linked together, and to Cape Town, by an excellent road and frequent rail services. Take the slow train along the scenic coastline from Muizenberg to Simon's Town – one of the most stunning train trips in the world – and stop for lunch at the Brass Bell restaurant, perched on the water's edge at Kalk Bay.

Simon's Town ★★★

This substantial and handsome bayside centre is steeped in naval history: it was founded by and named after the energetic Cape governor, Simon van der Stel, in 1687. The harbour provided a valuable anchorage during the Dutch colonial era and, after the British formally took over in 1814, served as the Royal Navy's main South Atlantic base.

It's still very much a naval town but not exclusively so. Commercial and leisure craft crowd the harbour (the **False Bay Yacht Club** is headquartered here), souvenir and craft shops abound. The local beaches are very enticing: **Seaforth, Foxy** Beach and their surrounds offer attractive stretches of sand and inlets; **Boulders** Beach is famous for its colony of endangered and endearing African penguins.

History, though, is the focus. More than 21 of the buildings that line the main street started life over 150 years ago (which is old for South Africa); much of the past has been preserved in

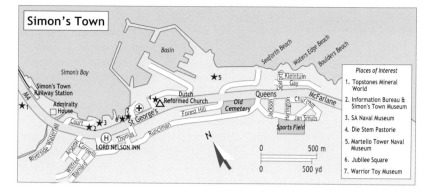

Simon's Town

Basin

Seaforth Beach
Waters Edge Beach
Boulders Beach

Simon's Bay

Simon's Town Railway Station

Admiralty House

Dutch Reformed Church

Old Cemetery

Forest Hill

Kleintuin Gay

Queens

McFarlane

Churchill

Jackson

Harrington

Jan Smuts

Sports Field

St George's

Court

LORD NELSON INN

Thomas

Runciman

Riverside Waterfall

Arsenal

Cornwall

Wilfred

Barnard

N

0   500 m
0   500 yd

Places of Interest

1. Topstones Mineral World
2. Information Bureau & Simon's Town Museum
3. SA Naval Museum
4. Die Stem Pastorie
5. Martello Tower Naval Museum
6. Jubilee Square
7. Warrior Toy Museum

the various museums; a Saturday morning guided walk through Simon's Town's **Historical Mile** leaves from the railway station to finish up at East Dock Yard (booking is advisable).

The splendid **Old Residency** (which is now home to the Simon's Town Museum) was built in 1777 as the governor's out-of-town hideaway or weekend retreat. Later, it did successive duty as slave quarters, a prison and a hospital and is now a showcase of interesting naval memorabilia – including mementos of Lord Nelson and a mock-up of a World War II pub – and various cultural collections.

One of the more appealing of the Residency's displays relates to **Just Nuisance**, the beloved Great Dane dog who befriended British sailors during World War II. During his lifetime he was formally ranked as an Able Seaman; on his death he was buried, with full military honours, on a hill overlooking town. A bronze statue of the dog stands in **Jubilee Square**.

Ships, sailors and the sea are also featured, in somewhat greater depth, in the **South African Naval Museum** on West Dockyard. Here there are dioramas of the town and its docks, insights into the realm of coastal defence and much else. Of quite different appeal is the **Warrior Toy Museum** in St George's Street, where you'll find an intriguing display of dolls, lead soldiers, miniature cars and trains.

THE NAME OF SIMON

The little naval settlement of Simon's Town, often referred to as Simonstown, was first known as Simon's Vlek after Dutch governor Simon van der Stel, who oversaw the colony from 1677 to 1699 and realized that the bay here would provide a safe harbour during the winter months. While its early years proved uneventful, it came unto its own when it played an important role as southern African base for the British navy. During the Second British Occupation, it became the home base of the South Atlantic Squadron, and one of the tasks that befell these men was to tend to the needs of Napoleon Bonaparte who had been exiled to the island of St Helena about 2000km (1200 miles) away in the South Atlantic Ocean. As a Royal Naval Base, tiny Simon's Town was finally on the map.

Just outside Simon's Town, up Dido Valley Road, you'll find **Topstones Mineral World**, reputed to be the world's biggest gemstone tumbling factory. Here you can watch huge quantities of rough stone converted into polished sparklers, which are then drilled and fashioned into jewellery and souvenirs. Visitors, especially children, are also invited to visit the cave and fossick in the scratch patch – a large heap of fragments. What you select you can keep, for a small fee.

Fish Hoek ★★

A solidly respectable seaside town (one of the only 'dry' municipalities in South Africa: no alcohol can be sold within its bounds), Fish Hoek is noted chiefly for its fine family beach and the warm summertime offshore waters bright with yachts, sailboards and catamarans. The gentle **Jager Walk**, along the shoreline rocks, fills a pleasant hour. The rock pools are very popular with young children. High above the valley that forms the 'waist' of the Peninsula is the celebrated **Peers Cave**, an important archaeological site and, some 15,000 years ago, home to Fish Hoek Man. The walls are decorated with prehistoric paintings and there are lovely views from the summit – although the climb is for the relatively fit.

The **Fish Hoek Valley Museum** has an informative Peers Cave exhibition as well as other displays relating to the archaeology and natural history of the broader area.

Above: *The beach at Fish Hoek, one of False Bay's larger towns. Jager Walk is a pleasant seafront stroll.*

Kalk Bay ★★

Kalk Bay is an enchanting little harbour and resort village further up the coast. 'Kalk' is the Afrikaans word for 'lime', and the bay was so named because all the shells

Left: *The pretty little village and harbour of Kalk Bay is the venue for a busy quayside fish market. The hills behind are cut through by labyrinthine caves.*

> ### FRESH FISH ON SALE
>
> At around noon each day **Kalk Bay's** little fishing boats return to harbour laden with the fruits of the sea, which are then auctioned off in lively and good-humoured fashion from the quayside. The prices are attractively low, and you can have your fish cleaned on the spot, fresh and ready to take home for the traditional South African *braai* (barbecue).

collected along the coast were burnt there to provide whitewash and mortar for colonial buildings. Today the main commercial activity is fishing; catches are sold on the quayside. The place is especially lively during June and July, when the snoek are running. Along the Main Road and alleys in the village are antique, pottery and junk shops, art galleries and restaurants.

Just behind the coastline, between the village and Muizenberg, are the Kalk Bay mountains, a modest but scenically striking range of hills cut through by a labyrinth of underground chambers. Many have odd-ball names (Mirth Parlour, Dolly's Doorway, Light and Gloom, Creepy Corridor), and they're worth exploring, though it's suggested you do so with someone who knows their way around. The wild and rocky area is also a magnet for hikers, ramblers, bird-spotters and lovers of nature.

The Muizenberg Area ★

A century ago Capetonian gentlefolk and the millionaire holiday-makers from the goldfields of the north flocked to what was then one of the southern hemisphere's premier seaside resorts. **Cecil Rhodes**, Cape premier, financial wizard and megalomaniac

False Bay

- Lakeside
- Zandvlei Bird Sanctuary
- Silvermine Nature Reserve
- Muizenberg
- Rhodes Cottage
- St James
- Kalk Bay
- Fish Hoek

False Bay

- Elsies Bay
- Glencairn
- Simon's Town
- Seaforth
- The Boulders
- Froggy Pond

Table Mountain National Park

0   2 km
0   1 mile

N

Above: *Muizenberg is famed for its long, broad white sands and its rather old-fashioned charm. The coast is very popular with surfers and fishermen.*

SEASIDE STROLL

Attractive features of **St James** are its gaily painted Victorian-type wooden bathing huts, its safe tidal pool, sheltered beach and rock pools bright with marine life. There is a very pleasant 3km (2-mile) walkway leading along the shoreline to **Muizenberg**. Points of interest en route (along Main Road and reached via a subway) include Rhodes Cottage and the Rust en Vrede mansion, designed by the celebrated architect Sir Herbert Baker in Cape Dutch Revival style. Die Posthuys, which is a whitewashed cottage, and Muizenberg railway station, are proclaimed national monuments.

empire-builder, died in 1902 in his small, plain, thatch-roofed, stone-walled holiday cottage just off the Main Road between **St James** (also worth a visit for its attractive bathing huts, tidal pool and lovely beach) and Muizenberg. The house has been preserved as a museum; old photographs and personal memorabilia recall the life and times of one of colonial South Africa's most controversial figures.

Closer to **Muizenberg** along Main Road is **Die Posthuys**, dating back to 1673 (making it the country's oldest European house), which served then as a signal house and small fort.

The town's genteel past is reflected in the Victorian villas, Edwardian boarding houses, renovated cottages and the imposing edifice of the railway station designed by Sir Herbert Baker. The candy-striped pavilion offers swimming, a water slide and a miniature golf course.

Another of Rhodes's friends, Rudyard Kipling, wrote evocatively of the 'white sands of Muizenberg, spun before the gale' and indeed the beach is special: a broad, long, gently sloping expanse of pale sand rhythmically pounded by long lines of breakers. Surfers love the place; so do board-sailors, yachtsmen, water-skiers and dog-walkers. Colourful bathing huts line the beach. There are plans to redevelop much of the beachfront and recapture Muizenberg's former glory.

Further down the coast you'll find some of the bigger beaches – specifically, **Sunrise** and **Mnandi** – but this section of the seaboard is quite undeveloped. It does, though, serve the high-density areas of the Cape Flats, and recreational amenities are improving.

Left: *Silvermine Nature Reserve offers some attractive walking trails.*

POSTAL PIONEER

Muizenberg's post office was the first in Africa to receive airmail: on 27 December 1911 South African pilot **Evelyn Driver**, a superb 'instinctive navigator' who had earlier helped pioneer Britain's Royal Mail Aerial Service, delivered 729 specially designed postcards from the Cape Town suburb of Kenilworth. The 12.8km (8-mile) flight, in a Bleriot monoplane, lasted seven and a half minutes. Muizenberg's second post office was built a few doors down in 1934.

The noted **Silvermine Nature Reserve** extends inland from the Muizenberg area. On the northern side of town is a delightful stretch of water called **Sandvlei**, favoured haunt of canoeists and water-sport enthusiasts. The eye-catching waterfront suburb of **Marina da Gama** flanks the lake's eastern shore.

Also north of Sunrise beach, in the low-lying, sandy terrain between suburb and coastal dune, is a scatter of shallow lakes cherished for their bird life. Well worth a visit is the **Rondevlei Nature Reserve** (Perth Road, Grassy Park), home to 225 different species, most of them waterfowl. Notables include the Caspian terns, the martial eagle and the African fish eagle. A few hippos hide away among the reeds. Hides, lookout towers equipped with telescopes, a waterfront walkway and a very interesting museum feature among the facilities.

ANNUAL EVENTS (CAPE TOWN AND PENINSULA)

Jan: The Minstrel (Coon) Carnival (New Year); J&B Met (Cape's top horse race); South Atlantic Race (previously known as Cape-to-Rio yacht race – every three years); Shakespeare season (at Maynardville Open-air Theatre).
Feb: Community Chest Carnival (at Maynardville).
Mar: University of Cape Town Rag Week; Cape Argus Pick 'n Pay Cycle Tour; Cape Town Festival; Navy Festival.
Apr: Old Mutual Two Oceans Marathon (Easter Sat).
May: Whale-watching season begins; Food & Wine Festival; Cape Gourmet Festival.
Jun/Jul: Berg River Canoe Marathon.
Jul/Aug: Hout Bay Snoek Derby.
Sep: Spring Wild Flower Shows; Whale-watching at its peak; Wine Festival.
Oct: International Film Festival.
Nov: Dragon Boat Festival.
Dec: Mother City Queer Project (gay festival); Christmas Carols.
For more events visit: www.tourismcapetown.co.za

5
Central Peninsula

The Peninsula's inland reaches – those that lie to the west of the suburban rail line – are hilly and well treed. The woodlands are at their densest and most enchanting on the **Constantiaberg** and in the valleys that sweep down from the southern part of Table Mountain.

The main inland motorway (the M3, which starts off as De Waal Drive and then undergoes several name changes: Rhodes Drive, Paradise, Edinburgh and finally called the Simon van der Stel highway) runs through the southern suburbs. These are heavily populated but still the route is for the most part a scenic delight.

GROOTE SCHUUR

The original Groote Schuur Estate (renamed Genadendal by Nelson Mandela), bequeathed to the nation by 19th-century politician and tycoon Cecil Rhodes, covers the mountain slopes beneath Devil's Peak and extends over parts of the Observatory, Mowbray, Rosebank and Rondebosch residential areas. Its most noteworthy component is perhaps the **Groote Schuur** ('Great Barn') homestead itself, which began life in the mid-1600s as Van Riebeeck's granary and, after a chequered career, was redesigned in imposing, though essentially simple, style by the turn-of-the-century architect Herbert Baker. It is for occupation by the president, if he so chooses.

More accessible, and more visible, is the **University of Cape Town**, the country's oldest and arguably most attractive. The ivy-covered buildings of its upper campus hug the hillside overlooking the highway; its medical

MEDICAL BREAKTHROUGH

Groote Schuur Hospital was the venue of the world's first human heart transplant. In 1967 Prof. **Christiaan Barnard** and his cardiac team implanted the heart of a 25-year-old accident victim into a middle-aged patient, **Louis Washkansky**, who, battling the effects of anti-rejection drugs, lived for just 18 more days before succumbing to pneumonia. Nevertheless the operation was considered a success.

Opposite: *Superb vistas from Rhodes Memorial.*

Right: *Rhodes Memorial is a monument to Cecil John Rhodes, who bequeathed his land to the people of South Africa.*

CAMPUS COUNT

- **University of the Western Cape** in Bellville was founded in 1960, during the apartheid years, to serve the Coloured community; it now has a mixed enrolment of about 14,000 students.
- **University of Cape Town** (UCT) has an enrolment of about 19,000.

Central Peninsula

school is housed in nearby Groote Schuur Hospital where, in 1967, Chris Barnard and his cardiac team performed the world's first human heart transplant operation.

For tea, scones and a quiet, relaxing hour in the loveliest of surrounds, take the **Rhodes Memorial** off-ramp just beyond the university. This leads around and back up the mountain-side to the unashamedly Imperialistic 'temple' that commemorates a man who, whatever his faults, strode like a Colossus across the Victorian colonial scene. The grand neoclassical structure, also the work of Herbert Baker, incorporates a powerful piece of statuary entitled 'Physical Energy' by FG Watts, together with the four pairs of lion-sphinxes and a bust of Rhodes by JW Swan, beneath which is inscribed Kipling's moving tribute to 'the immense and brooding spirit'.

Observatory and Rosebank ★

The first of these suburbs took its name from the Royal (now the South African National) Observatory, established in 1821 in what was then a wilderness infested by snakes, hippos and leopards.

Further along, on Rosebank's Cecil Road, is the **Irma Stern Museum**, which features the works of one of the country's most prolific and controversial artists. Stern gave the first of her many one-woman shows in Berlin in 1919 but on her return to South Africa her rich, sensual canvases were dismissed as 'revolutionary' (and even immoral), and it wasn't until the 1930s that she began to gain local acceptance. She died in 1966. On display in her Rosebank home, The Firs, are some 200 of her paintings, together with sculptures and her fine collection of antiques, *objets d'art* and African artefacts brought back from the Congo (DRC).

Among other elements of the original estate in Main Road, Rondebosch, are the **Baxter Theatre Complex** (*see* page 22) and **Mostert's Mill**, a traditional Dutch windmill (it is one of only two in the Cape) on De Waal Drive. The mill, which dates from 1796, has been carefully restored and is open to the public. Rondebosch is a university suburb, with many students living in 'digs' in the area.

Newlands ★★

This sprawling, fashionable suburb, about 6km (4 miles) from the city centre, is noted for its densely treed avenues, its international **cricket** and **rugby** grounds, and its unusually high rainfall – the product of wind patterns and the high mountain backdrop.

For rugby enthusiasts, especially, Newlands is something of a mecca. The stadium hosted the opening match of the 1995 World Cup, among the latest of a long sequence of significant contests stretching back to 1891, when WE Maclagen led the first British team onto a South African field (the tourists conceded just one try in a series of 19 games played countrywide). In the decades that followed, South Africa reached and maintained a pre-eminent position in international rugby until its enforced isolation during the wilderness years of apartheid. Much of the story is told by the **South African Rugby Museum**, largest of its kind in the world.

On the Liesbeeck River close to the stadium is the **Josephine Mill**, built in 1840,

THE HOME OF RUGBY

Newlands Rugby Stadium is the historic and handsome venue for provincial and international matches and was host for the opening ceremony of the 1995 **Rugby World Cup**, which the national Springbok side went on to win. A frequent suburban train service ferries spectators directly to the 50,000-capacity arena. The country's major provincial competition is the **Currie Cup**, contested by the regional unions. Of these, the top five go on to take part in the southern hemisphere's 'Super 14' tournament comprising teams from South Africa, New Zealand and Australia.

THE GENTLER GAME

Sahara Park Newlands, with its stately oak and plane trees and Table Mountain backdrop, is among the world's most attractive cricket pitches. Here, on lazy summer days, you can watch four-day provincial matches and occasional five-day tests against a touring side. Cricket of a different, more lively kind is on view during the one-day internationals and the day-night provincial series (known informally as the 'pyjama game' for the bright team colours worn by the players). Match details are published in local newspapers.

named in honour of the Crown Princess of Sweden, who later became queen, and now Cape Town's only surviving watermill. There are guided tours and daily milling demonstrations (wholewheat flour is produced in much the same way as it was 150 years ago, and flour and biscuits are for sale), a restaurant and pleasant tea garden.

Sunday concerts are held outdoors at the mill in summer (November to February) starting at 17:30.

Off the M3 highway, to your right as you drive away from the city (after the University of Cape Town), you'll see the tall trees of **Newlands forest**, a delightful place for picnics and barbecues and much favoured by brisk walkers, hikers and joggers.

Claremont and Wynberg ★

Claremont, one of the country's fastest-growing commercial centres, is especially enticing: its sophisticated **Cavendish Square** and **Cavendish Connect** complexes offer a kaleidoscope of all-purpose stores, speciality outlets, excellent restaurants, snack bars, bistros and cinemas. **The Arderne Gardens** in Main Road, Claremont, are also worth a visit – for their magnificent exotic trees (cedars, cypresses, Norfolk pines among others) and for the fragile delicacy of their Japanese section.

Wynberg is known for its **Village**, a charming cluster of pre-1850 Chelsea-style cottages and antique shops. The nearby **Maynardville Open-air Theatre** is a well-patronized venue for Shakespearean productions during January and February, as well as the annual **Community Chest Carnival,** a fund-raising event that features the food and music of the Cape's many cultures.

THE CONSTANTIA AREA

Constantia is not so much a suburb as a semirural and rather lovely swathe of valley, hill, wooded parkland and smart homes hidden discreetly among the trees. It is a very sought-after residential area. The valley also sustained South Africa's first vineyards (*see* page 13), and its historic estates enjoy an honourable place in the world of wine.

Kirstenbosch ★★★

The gardens that sprawl over some 530ha (1310 acres) of Table Mountain's well-watered southern slopes were founded in 1913 to preserve and propagate South Africa's rich floral heritage, and are today recognized as one of the world's most respected botanical enterprises.

> **LADY ANNE'S LEGACY**
>
> Lady Anne Barnard was one of London's best hostesses – she numbered Dr Samuel Johnson, William Pitt and the Prince of Wales among her friends – before her arrival in 1797, soon after the first British Occupation (her husband, Andrew, had been appointed colonial secretary at the Cape). Her charm and natural diplomacy did much to win the locals over to the new regime, but her main gifts to posterity were the journal she kept, and the many letters she wrote describing the people of and life in the new colony. Both the journal and the letters were embellished with her skilful sketches. Her beautiful Newlands home, built in 1799, is now the famous Vineyard Hotel.

The grounds embrace about half the country's 18,000 species of flowering plant, among them the proteas and ericas of the Cape's unique *fynbos* vegetation (*see* page 8): disas, bulbs, succulents, ferns, pelargoniums (the stock from which geraniums have been hybridized to decorate the window-boxes of five continents) and the fascinating, primeval cycads.

The greater proportion of this floral wealth can be seen in the relatively small (160ha; 395-acre) cultivated section. Of special note is the **Cycad Ampitheatre**; sanctuary for most of southern Africa's 20-odd species (falling into two genera) of a plant type that first appeared 150 million years ago to reach its ascendancy about 80 million years later, during the last age of the dinosaurs (*see* panel, page 8).

A SUMMER GARDEN

The gardens of **Kirstenbosch** are attractive all year round but are best in spring (September and October), when the annuals and many proteas are in bloom, and the bird life at its most animated.

Jazz and other outdoor concerts enliven summer Sunday evenings. Guided tours are offered during the week. The gardens have been enhanced by an impressive Visitor's Centre, incorporating an information office, book-and-souvenir shop, restaurant, and modern Glass House conservatory.

Above right: *The floral delights of Kirstenbosch.*
Opposite: *A refreshing halt on the drive through the scenic Constantia area.*
Below: *Proteas feature strongly at Kirstenbosch.*

The cultivated area is logically arranged in a series of informal spreads that include, among much else, the **Protea Gardens** and the succulents of the **JW Matthews Rock Garden**. Meandering between these specialized sections are pathways that invite the leisurely stroller. For the visually disabled, there's a **perfume garden** and a **braille walk**.

Of modest historical interest are the remains of a wild almond hedge planted in 1660 (to keep the first Dutch settlement's cattle from being stolen), and a charming little pool, built with Batavian brick, in the shape of a bird.

Kirstenbosch is primarily a research centre; intense study and meticulous documentation are undertaken in the on-site **Compton Herbarium**, repository of more than 250,000 botanical specimens. Some of the items belong to now-extinct species.

Constantia Nek ★★

The scenic route along **Rhodes Avenue** (M63) from Kirstenbosch up to Constantia Nek – the summit of a pass that links the Hout Bay and Constantia valleys – is a visual joy, as the road winds through a fantasia of trees, ferns and flowers. On your right is the **Cecilia forest** which is popular among Capetonian walkers, ramblers and those who feel the need to commune with gentler spirits. The effort needed to reach the waterfall is worthwhile.

At the top of the Nek (where there's a pleasant restaurant), the route divides: the road to the right leads to Hout Bay (see page 54), that to the left takes you down into Constantia proper and its three time-honoured and graceful Cape Dutch homesteads.

Groot Constantia ★★★

The lime-washed, gabled and beautifully thatched mansion, perhaps the country's stateliest, was originally conceived and built, and its first vineyards laid out, in 1685 by Cape governor **Simon van der Stel** (see page 13), who happily spent his declining years there. His ghost, it is said, still walks the oak-lined avenue that leads to an ornamental pool where the local aristocracy once disported themselves.

In 1778 Groot Constantia was bought by the wealthy Cloete family, who had an eye for beauty as well as a gift for wine-making (Constantia products were praised by, among others, Napoleon, Bismarck and Louis Philippe of France). In 1791 **Hendrik Cloete**, the patriarch, added a splendid two-storeyed cellar designed by the French architect Louis Thibault. Its pediment is decorated by sculptor Anton Anreith with a stucco relief of Ganymede, cup-bearer to the Grecian gods, and a bevy of cavorting cherubs. The cellar is now a museum that tells the story of wine and wine-making through the ages.

The main house burned down in 1925, but restoration work over the years has been meticulous, and the place still looks very much as it did at the height of its glory. Inside, you'll find period furniture, tapestries, paintings, exquisite porcelain (Delft, Rhineland, Chinese and Japanese) and *objets d'art*.

Nearby is the **Jonkershuis** (the Dutch word for 'young gentleman's house'), a kind of annexe which, in the early days and among the more affluent Dutch landowners, was reserved for the family's eldest son.

ELEGANCE AT ALPHEN

A historic **Constantia** homestead that does not feature on the formal 'wine route', but is well worth visiting, is **Alphen**, located on an estate first farmed in 1714. The stately double-storeyed Cape Dutch house, which dates from 1753, now functions as a country hotel noted for its superbly proportioned rooms, high beamed ceilings, leaded-light windows and its wealth of antiques, oil paintings and *objets d'art*. Some of the guest rooms open out onto pleasant courtyards. **The Winery** is a showpiece, and the cellar is well stocked with award-winning vintages. The Boer and the Brit is the cozy pub.

Above: *Historic Groot Constantia, oldest and stateliest of the Peninsula's homesteads. Its vineyards, first planted in 1685, continue to yield fine wines.*

Groot Constantia houses three restaurants. Traditional Cape fare is served in the Jonkershuis; the **Tavern** offers buffet lunches, bench seating and a sociable, rather Germanic atmosphere whilst Simon's is an a la carte restaurant. Many visitors, though, prefer to bring along a picnic hamper and relax on the shade-dappled lawns. A watchtower gives a bird's-eye view of the vineyards. There are tours of the modern cellar, wine tastings and sales for those who want to invest in a bottle or two, an art gallery and souvenir shop.

The Smaller Homesteads ★★

Groot Constantia is one of five working estates that, together, comprise the Peninsula's only 'wine route'. More modest but just as eye-catching in its own way is **Klein Constantia**, built in 1796 and rescued from years of neglect, and quite beautifully renovated, by Capetonian Douglas Jooste. It's a rather private place, but one can tour the modern cellars (they have won design awards) by appointment and purchase wine.

Klein Constantia's Vin de Constance is extremely popular in exclusive French restaurants.

Nearby is **Buitenverwachting** (which means 'beyond expectations'), an impressive complex of gabled house, cellars, slave quarters and stables that have been faultlessly restored. The estate runs one of the Western Cape's

---

TASTING TIMES

• **Groot Constantia:** Markets about 17 wines. Tastings and sales. Tours are held hourly between 10:00 and 16:00 daily except Good Friday, Christmas and New Year's Day; tel: (021) 794-5128. Restaurants:
• **Jonkershuis,** tel: (021) 794-6255; **Simon's,** tel: (021) 794-2984.
• **Klein Constantia:** Tastings and sales 09:00–17:00 Mon–Fri, 09:00–13:00 Sat; tours by appointment; tel: (021) 794-5188.
• **Buitenverwachting:** Tastings and sales 09:00–17:00 Mon–Fri; 09:00–13:00 Sat. The restaurant, one of the Cape's best, is open Mon–Fri for lunch and dinner, Sat for dinner only (Café Petite is open for lunch); tel: (021) 794-3522.

• **Steenberg:** Sales 09:00–16:30 Mon–Fri, 09:30–13:30 Sat; cellar tours by appointment; tel: (021) 713-2211.The restaurant, Catharina's, is open daily from 07:30 for breakfast, lunch and dinner, tel: (021) 713-2222.
• **Constantia Uitsig:** Tasting and sales 09:00–16:00 Mon–Fri, 10:00–15:30 Sat, Sun; tel: (021) 794-1810. The estate boasts two of the most stylish restaurants on the Peninsula and a café: Constantia Uitsig, open for lunch 12:00–14:30 and dinner from 19:00, tel: (021) 794-4480; La Colombe, open for lunch 12:30–17:00 and dinner from 19:30, tel: (021) 794-2390; Spaanchemat River Café, breakfast and lunch only, tel: (021) 794-3010.

best restaurants, and produces some of its best wines (many releases have won international acclaim). Again, cellar tours are conducted by appointment; tastings and sales are a daily feature.

The oldest of all the farms is **Steenberg**, on the corner of Steenberg and Tokai roads. Steenberg Farm was granted to Catharina Ras (Ustings) in 1682, the title deed formally signed by Simon van der Stel in 1688. The farm was later owned by Russouws and then the Louws and finally purchased in 1990 by Johannesburg Consolidated Investment Company. Steenberg produces wine of superior quality; visits and sales by appointment.

Constantia Uitsig has 30 hectares under vine and only produces 17 000 cases of superior wine a year. (Cellar tours and wine tasting can be done by appointment.)

Silvermine Nature Reserve ★

This pristine 2000ha (4942-acre) wilderness extends over the **Steenberg hills**, and across the narrow waist of the Peninsula, from **Kalk Bay** and **Muizenberg** in the east to **Noordhoek** in the west. The fynbos flora was devastated by fire in January 2000 but has made a remarkable recovery, its new growth graced by some brand-new species. The terrain is rugged, an attractive compound of mountain peak, plateau and forested gorge, upland stream, waterfall and, everywhere, an astonishing floral diversity. Bird life is prolific.

A network of safe paths has been laid out; charted walks take in viewpoints and picnic spots (many of which you can also drive or mountainbike to). Magnificent coast-to-coast views unfold along the route to the heights above the reservoir.

Silvermine – early Dutch settlers dug the slopes for the precious metal, though without success – is bisected by the scenically entrancing **Ou Kaapse Weg** that leads south-west to Sun Valley. The drive is thoroughly recommended.

THE OLD CAPE ROAD

Ou Kaapse Weg ('Old Cape Road', or the M64) is a fine scenic drive that cuts through **Silvermine**, running south-west from the **Westlake** area to climb over the **Steenberg** ('stony mountain') plateau before descending to **Fish Hoek** valley and **Noordhoek** on the west coast. Along the winding way are a myriad indigenous flowers that are at their colourful best in springtime, and splendid views across the southern Peninsula. Among the most eye-catching vistas is that from just below the entrance to the Silvermine section of Table Mountain National Park.

Below: *One of many contour paths through Silvermine Nature Reserve.*

6
The Winelands

Beyond the bleak Cape Flats, to the north and east of Cape Town, the land rises to the splendid upland ranges of the coastal rampart. The mountains – part of what is known as the Cape fold mountains – are high, their lower slopes and the valleys in between are green and fertile, mantled by pastures and orchards and, especially, by vineyards heavy with fruit.

The Winelands were the first of the country areas to be occupied by the early white settlers. As the farmers flourished so they established villages and, from the later 1600s, began enlarging and beautifying their homes. The first houses were modest but, with prosperity, took on wings and cellars, lofts, slave quarters and courtyards.

THE WINE ROUTES

Perhaps the most enjoyable way of exploring this region is via various wine routes – wine-tasting and sightseeing itineraries inspired by and modelled on the successful *weinstrassen* of Germany and France's *routes de vin*.

There are around thirteen of these wine-ways, collectively covering the ground from the Cape Peninsula (Constantia: *see* page 73) northeast as far as Worcester and Robertson, east to take in the Little Karoo, and up the western coastal belt, where the Swartland and Olifantsrivier wineries attract an ever-increasing number of visitors. Three routes, however, are pre-eminent in the Winelands proper.

The **Stellenbosch Wine Route** was the first to be established (in 1971). Today it embraces more than 300

CAPE DUTCH STYLE

Cape Dutch architecture is unique in character. It evolved over a century and has many variations. But the Winelands' mansions share common elements: thick, whitewashed walls, thatched roofs, and an elegant symmetry of line. The focal point is the imposing central entrance, flanked by evenly spaced shuttered windows and surmounted by an impressive gable. The front door leads into the *voorkamer* (front room), which is often divided from the *agterkamer* (rear room) by an elaborate wooden screen (folded to either side for entertaining).

Opposite: *The vineyards of Franschhoek Valley.*

PUBS AND TAVERNS

Stellenbosch, with its large student population, is especially well served by pubs and taverns. Most offer inexpensive pub lunches, and some serve full meals, provide live music and stay open till late. Among the more popular are:
• **De Akker**, Dorp Street, tel: (021) 883-3512. A wine-tasting centre as well as a favourite pub of students. Next door is the renowned Oom Samie se Winkel trading store.
• **De Kelder**, Dorp Street, (021) 883-3797. À la carte Austrian cuisine.
• **Jan Cats**, Andringa Street, tel: (021) 887-3644. Part of the historic Stellenbosch Hotel.

Above: *La Concorde, headquarters of KWV.*
Below: *Indulgent wine tasting at Nederburg.*

wine and grape producers, some of them centuries old, their Cape Dutch homesteads a delight to the eye. Nearby **Franschhoek**, in the lovely valley of that name, offers 26 venues, most with names reflecting their French Huguenot origins. The **Paarl Vintners** has 26 full members and also offers the full spectrum of wines; from light whites to full-bodied reds, ports and sherries – and one or two especially notable venues (including the giant KWV wine enterprise and Nederburg: *see* page 95).

The wine routes are well signposted with their distinctive emblems. Most of the cellars offer tastings and tours; some run restaurants with sophisticated menus (traditional Cape dishes feature prominently), others offer simple fare of the 'vintner's or cheese platter'; at still others you'll find a small museum, a gallery, or a farm stall that sells home-made preserves, fruit and cheeses.

Visitors are cordially received. The growers are proud of their vineyards and vintages, and will talk revealingly of the subtleties and secrets of wine-making. The tours are leisurely affairs during which you take in the bottling and labelling processes and the tiered casks stored away in the dim coolness of a wine- and wood-scented cellar.

STELLENBOSCH ★★★

South Africa's second oldest town, founded in 1679 and named in honour of Simon van der Stel, lies in the green and pleasant Eerste ('first') River Valley beneath the heights of the **Papegaaiberg**, or 'parrot mountain'. The place wears its age with grace: the early towns-folk planted oak trees, created open spaces, built churches and charming little lime-washed homes; later generations added statelier private residences, some fine public edifices and a university.

Above: *Quaint Cape farmstead.*

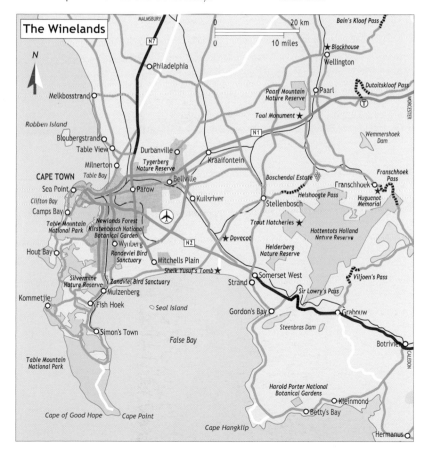

The Winelands

N

MALMSBURY

0   20 km

0   10 miles

Bain's Kloof Pass

Philadelphia

N7

Blockhouse

Wellington

Melkbosstrand

Paarl Mountain
Nature Reserve

Paarl

Dutoitskloof Pass

WORCESTER

Taal Monument ★

Robben Island

N1

Wemmershoek
Dam

Bloubergstrand

Table View

Durbanville

Kraaifontein

Tygerberg
Nature Reserve

Boschendal Estate

Franschhoek

Franschhoek
Pass

Milnerton

Table Bay

Bellville

CAPE TOWN

Sea Point

Parow

Kuilsriver

Helshoogte Pass

Huguenot
Memorial

Clifton Bay

Stellenbosch

Camps Bay

Table Mountain
National Park

Newlands Forest
Kirstenbosch National
Botanical Garden

Wynberg

N2

Dovecot ★

Trout Hatcheries ★

Hottentots Holland
Nature Reserve

Hout Bay

Rondevlei Bird
Sanctuary

Mitchells Plain

Helderberg
Nature Reserve

Sheik Yusuf's Tomb ★

Silvermine
Nature Reserve

Zandvlei Bird Sanctuary

Somerset West

Viljoen's Pass

Kommetjie

Muizenberg

Strand

Fish Hoek

Seal Island

Sir Lowry's Pass

Gordon's Bay

Grabouw

Simon's Town

False Bay

Steenbras Dam

CALEDON

Botrivier

Table Mountain
National Park

Harold Porter National
Botanical Gardens

Kleinmond

Cape of Good Hope

Cape Point

Betty's Bay

Cape Hangklip

Hermanus

CAMPUS DRAWCARDS

Stellenbosch University is not confined within a single location: campus and town are integrated, which tends to create a refreshing air of youthfulness and verve in the restaurants, pubs, shops, streets and parks. Among the institution's drawcards are some fine buildings; the **Dorp Street Art Gallery** (corner of Dorp and Bird streets); the **Sasol Art Museum** (Ryneveld Street), which houses the university's permanent collection and stages regular cultural displays, and the attractive botanical gardens.

Today, the thoroughfares of the town are still lined with massive oaks – hence the Afrikaans name 'Eikestad' ('town of oaks'). Much else of the past also remains. The legacy is strikingly visible in and around the town centre, which embraces around 60 national heritage monuments. Many may be found in **Dorp Street**, which boasts the country's largest row of historic buildings.

Places from the Past

Four splendid houses, representing different eras, have been faithfully restored to their original glory and now form Stellenbosch's **Village Museum**, a complex that illuminates the changing domestic scene during the 18th and much of the 19th centuries. Each is furnished in period fashion, its garden filled with the kinds of plants – decorative, medicinal and culinary – that the early owners would have cultivated. The oldest of the houses is

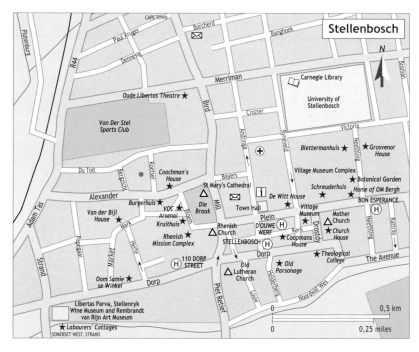

Schreuderhuis, built in 1709 by a German immigrant, its architecture, décor and simple, rough-hewn furniture matching his humble status. Much grander is **Blettermanhuis**, which is typical of the late 18th century. **Grosvenor House**, the kind of town house built by patrician Cape families of the early 1800s, is the most elegant of the four, and its garden the most interesting (it houses a permanent exhibition entitled 'Toys of Yesteryear'). Finally there's the home of **OM Bergh**, dating from the latter part of the 19th century and Victorian in character.

Above: *The old Kruithuis in Stellenbosch, built as a powder magazine and arsenal in 1777.*

Restoration work is continuing, and the Village Museum is to be enlarged with the addition of two more houses, covering the Edwardian and 1920s periods.

You'll also find some noteworthy buildings around **Die Braak**, the spacious village green that once served both as a parade ground for the militia and as an arena for local festivities. Its military origins are evident in the nearby **Kruithuis** (arsenal), built in 1777 and now a national monument housing old weaponry and Dutch East India Company memorabilia. Other points of interest include the **Burgerhuis** (once the home of the magistrate and now a museum and the headquarters of the Historical Homes of South Africa); the delightful little thatch-roofed Anglican church of **St Mary's-on-the-Braak**, and the **Rhenish Mission** complex, whose church pulpit is one of the finest in the country.

In somewhat lighter vein, make a point of calling in at **Oom Samie se Winkel**, which translates as 'Uncle Sammy's Shop' and which first opened its doors for business during Stellenbosch's infancy. It's since been given a Victorian face-lift, complete with wrought-iron tracery, the interior crammed with home-made preserves, bric-a-brac, curios, bottles of good wine and much else. The scents that regale you – of spices and fresh fruit, tobacco,

WALKING THROUGH THE WINELANDS

Hikers and ramblers have a wide choice of routes through the Winelands: from strenuous scrambles over rugged slopes to gentle walks through the fertile farmlands, the **Jonkershoek Valley** and the **Assegaalbosch** and **Helderberg** reserves. Among the most enticing is the **Vineyard Trail**, a marked route that starts from Stellenbosch's **Oude Libertas Centre**, then up the **Papegaaiberg**, through forest plantations, orchards and vineyards to **Kuilsrivier** in the west. The full route is 24km (15 miles) long and takes a day to complete, but you can turn off after 7km (4.5 miles) and return to Stellenbosch through the exquisite **Devon Valley**.

Above: *Oom Samie's shop.*

dried fish and leather – belong to that long-gone, more leisurely age before the coming of supermarkets.

Part of Oom Samie se Winkel has been set aside as **The Victorian Wine Shop**, a cozy little corner that houses the region's best releases together with some unusual vintages. The staff will make up (and also despatch) gift packages for you. There's also a pleasant tea garden at the back. **De Akker**, a few steps along the road, is a lively pub and popular wine-tasting centre.

One of South Africa's earliest and most attractive inns is **D'Ouwe Werf** ('The Old Yard'), located on Church Street. The hotel has been welcoming guests for close on three centuries, though under different guises, and is a stylish place recently renovated in keeping with its venerable past. The best of the 25 rooms are sumptuously furnished with four-posters, magnificent antiques and opulent fabrics. Its restaurant, which has an entrancing outside area shaded by vine-covered pergolas, serves traditional Cape food, scrumptious home-made cakes, pastries and excellent coffee.

The World of Wine

As you can imagine, Stellenbosch has much to offer the wine-lover. Well worth visiting is **Libertas Parva Cellar**, an elegantly gabled Cape Dutch mansion that houses the massive vats, presses and old implements of the **Stellenryck Wine Museum**. Especially intriguing exhibits include the ancient Greek and Roman amphora, a jug from Biblical Israel, goblets and bottles from the early Dutch Cape and some fine examples of antique glassware. Next door, **Libertas Parva**, once home to the wife of statesman Jan Smuts and social

---

MUSIC IN THE AIR

On the southern fringes of Stellenbosch is the **Oude Libertas Centre**, which welcomes visitors to its underground cellar and restaurant. The centre is best known, however, for its Sunday evening concerts in its 430-seat amphitheatre, modelled on the auditoria of ancient Athens and Epidauros. Here you sit in the enclosure or on the surrounding lawns with a picnic hamper, sipping wine while the music washes over you – a magical experience. The concerts are held from December through to March, which are warm, dry and mostly wind-free months. The season's programme ranges through the spectrum from jazz and the joyous sounds of Africa to Brahms and Beethoven. Drama and ballet also feature occasionally.

venue for many South African political luminaries, has retained its period character. It also houses the well-known **Rembrandt van Rijn Art Museum** of works by some of the country's leading artists.

Some of the world's biggest wine vats can be seen in the coolness of the **Bergkelder**, a labyrinthine cellar complex tunnelled out of Stellenbosch's Papegaaiberg mountain.

The cloister-like, candle-lit, aromatic chambers are lined to their arched ceilings with tiered bottles; one section has been set aside as the Vinotèque (a place where wines owned by private individuals – mainly investors – are matured). Tours and tastings are offered.

Above: *Oak-lined Dorp Street in Stellenbosch was known as 'the wagon road to the Cape'. It has the country's longest row of historic buildings.*

Near Stellenbosch

The **Van Ryn Brandy Distillery** and maturation cellars, situated on the R310 in Vlottenburg Road to the south-west of town, are among the country's largest and most impressive. Guided tours of the facility take in tastings; audiovisuals, cooperage demonstrations and brandy courses are also offered.

At **Dombeya Farm** (off the R44 near Rust-en-Vrede wine estate), a worthwhile community weaving project turns out colourful fabrics, mats, shawls and jerseys made from locally spun wool. The farm is open 09:00–17:00 daily.

THE STELLENBOSCH WINE FARMS ★★★

The cellars and co-operatives are well worth visiting for their wines, ambience and the charming settings. The wine route is divided into five sub-routes: Greater Simonsberg, Stellenbosch Berg, Helderberg, Stellenbosch West and Bottelary Hills. An official guide of the

---

ANIMALS ON VIEW

The Western Cape is not big-game country, but you can catch a glimpse of South Africa's splendid wildlife heritage in the **Wiesenhof Game Reserve**, 12km (7 miles) north of Stellenbosch off the Paarl road (R44). Here the animals roam freely over the parkland (they're fed daily between 11:00 and noon). There's boating on the small lake, a roller-skating rink, swimming pools, picnic and barbecue spots, a coffee shop and other day-excursion attractions. Also worth visiting is **Drakenstein Lion Park**, where the animals can be viewed from a catwalk.

HEALTH HYDRO

If the good food and wine of the region threatens to take its toll, pay a visit to **The Hydro** in the attractive Idas Valley near Stellenbosch. Among South Africa's premier health resorts, The Hydro offers an invigorating and individually monitored regimen of massage, hydro- and heat therapy, water aerobics and much else, all enjoyed in luxurious surrounds. You really need to stay for a week or more to extract the maximum benefit from the routine and treatments, but The Hydro also caters for day visitors in search of a briefer stress-free retreat.

Light lunches (salad and vegetable buffet) are served; booking essential; tel: (021) 809-3800.

Stellenbosch Winelands

Klapmuts
Simonsvlei
Drakenstein
N1
Muldersvlei
Backsberg
Villiera
Koelenhof
Simondium
R304
Lievland
Kraaifontein
Simonsig
Kanonkop
M23
Muratie
Koelenhof
Delheim
Bottelary
Morgenhof
Hartenberg
Schoongezicht
Bertrams
Banhoek
Delaire
Uiterwyk
Neethlingshof
Stellenbosch
Goedgeloof
Vlottenburg
Zevenwacht
M12
Eersterivier Vallei
Lynedoch
Spier
Brandy Cellar
Blaauwklippen
Hottentots Holland
Nature Reserve
Welmoed
Rust en Vrede
Eikendal
De Helderberg
Helderberg
Nature Reserve
N
Macassar
Firgrove
N2
Macassar Beach
Somerset West
BOTRIVIER
0   4 km
0   2 miles

Opposite left: *The Delaire homestead.*
Opposite right: *Wooded hills and vineyards on the Morgenhof estate.*
Below: *The traditional Cape Dutch interior of Blaauwklippen Manor.*

wine farms is available from tourist information offices. Among the more prominent wine farms are:

Blaauwklippen, a classic H-shaped Cape Dutch mansion with intricately decorative gables. It's also a working, all-purpose farm. Among its eclectic attractions is a museum of coaches, carriages, vintage and veteran vehicles. During the summer months, there are tours of the vineyards by horse-drawn coach and a delicious 'coachman's lunch' is available at a reasonable price.

Delaire, situated high up on the Helshoogte pass, offers a small range of good wines, as well as lunches at the Green Door restaurant, picnics on the lawns in season and splendid views.

Delheim, a long-time stalwart on the wine route, is situated on the slopes of the Simonsberg. With good wines, alfresco eating and memorable vistas across to Table Mountain and the coast, Delheim's tasting room is a place for lingering.

Eikendal is on the Somerset West road, on the slopes of the Helderberg mountains. Quality classic wines from the Austrian- and SA-trained team. Daily lunches, based on Swiss country cuisine. Friday evening Swiss cheese fondues are a winter speciality.

Hartenberg, on the Bottelary road, offers an impressive line-up of wines from a young, dynamic team. Vintners lunches daily (except Sunday). Tastings and sales.

Hazendal, where a predominantly female team are busily shaping this estate's future direction. A new cellar sports the latest in technology, while the old cellar has become the tasting centre. Wine and music evenings at the restaurant in winter.

Morgenhof, on the R44, dates from 1692, the homestead from 1820. French-owned by the Huchon family, owners of Gosset champagne (est. 1584). New vineyards, barrel maturation cellar for whites and underground octagonal barrel cellar for reds all add up to an estate dedicated to quality. Light lunches all year round, picnics in summer.

Muratie, a fine Cape Dutch homestead, one of the region's oldest (est. 1685), is noted for its ports and red wines. Cellar tours by appointment.

Neethlingshof has a beautiful avenue of stone pines leading to a showpiece estate whose drawcards include the Lord Neethling restaurant and the more casual glass-enclosed Palm Terrace. The gabled house is famed for its exquisite grounds. Tastings and sales daily, farm tours with braai in summer, cellar tours on request.

Saxenburg, leading proponent of 'new wave' Cape wines, is situated on the slopes of the Bottelary Hill above Kuilsrivier. Range includes a SA-French blend, from grapes grown on the owner's properties in both countries. Tastings (Mon–Sat; Sun except July) are charged for. The restaurant (closed Jun–Aug) offers lunch (Wed–Mon) and dinner (Wed–Sat).

Simonsig is located between Stellenbosch and the N1. It comprises three original farms, dating from 1682. One of the largest Cape estates and the first in SA to produce a *méthode champenoise* sparkling wine. Cellar tours Mon–Sat. Tasting is charged for.

SPIER WINE ESTATE

This estate has been renovated and upgraded into a showpiece for the Cape Winelands. Attractions include wine tastings, a wine shop and a range of eating options (such as the Taphuis pub, Mojo, Figaro's, Toto's, or Jonkershuis restaurant). Picnic baskets are also for sale and visitors can wander in the attractive grounds, or take a trip in an old horse-drawn cart. There are also pony rides for children. The open-air amphitheatre offers live jazz, classical and light music in summer. A cheetah breeding project and bird of prey centre forms part of the property, as do stables. For a full day's outing, take the Spier Vintage train, departing from the Spier Monument Station in Cape Town.

Opposite: *The Huguenot Memorial, Franschhoek.*
Below: *Trout hatcheries in enchanting Jonkershoek.*

Uiterwyk has been in the same family since 1912. The homestead, built in 1791, is a national monument. Cellar tours by appointment.

Welmoed is on the R310 and the first winery on the route when approached from the N2. Cellar tours by appointment, but excellent wine-tasting and sales. The restaurant offers wholesome and filling lunches.

JONKERSHOEK VALLEY ★★

The **Eerste River** rises to the east of Stellenbosch, and flows through a hill-flanked countryside that beckons the hiker and lover of nature. Within the valley are the historic homesteads of **Oude Nektar** and **Lanzerac**; the latter is a neoclassical manor house that made its appearance in 1830 (though some of the outbuildings are much older) and which is now one of the region's best-known hotels. Guests approach the beautifully maintained complex along an avenue of stately plane trees. The outhouses have been converted into bed-rooms, the original wine cellar into the reception area and fine restaurant. Lanzerac also houses the informal Vinkel en Koljander restaurant, an art gallery and a small museum of Cape furniture.

Stellenbosch University's **Jonkershoek Fisheries Research Station**, which runs South Africa's oldest and largest hatcheries, breeds trout, bream and bass for release into rivers and dams throughout the country. The aquarium features local and some exotic freshwater fish.

Some 160ha (395 acres) of precious Cape mountain *fynbos* (heath-type) vegetation are protected within the valley's **Assegaaibosch Nature Reserve**. A variety of the proteas are both rare and eye-catching. A network of short walks has been laid out, together with picnic and barbecue sites and a small (5ha; 12-acre) wild-flower garden with specimens labelled for identification.

Further to the east is the much larger (400ha; 988-acre) **Hottentots Holland Nature Reserve**, a splendid area of mountains, gorges, dense woodlands and tumbling upland streams. This is a place for serious walkers (there's no access for cars), many of whom embark on the challenging Boland trail, a three-day, 41km (25-mile) route divided into shorter circular sections. If you're interested in wild flowers, keep an eye out for the rare marsh rose and the blushing bride. For the rest, there are forest-clad kloofs to explore, clear mountain pools to bathe in, and superb views over the countryside towards the coast.

FRANSCHHOEK ★★★

The town's name – it means 'French corner' – reflects its Gallic origins: it was founded in 1688 by a party of **Huguenot** émigrés, refugees from a Europe torn by the religious wars. There were not very many of them, and they were scattered among the resident Dutch and German freeburghers rather than allowed to form a separate community, so they soon lost their language and cultural identity. But they were hard-working and skilled folk, and they did much for the local wine industry – and the architecture of the region. As a legacy of their Huguenot past, many fine estates and homesteads still bear their original French names, among them **La Provence**, **La Motte**, **Haute Provence**, **La Couronne** and **L'Ormarins**.

The early French Huguenots and their legacy are commemorated in a very imposing, though delicately graceful, memorial and museum complex in Franschhoek. The monument is full of elaborate Christian symbolism – three elegant arches represent the Holy Trinity; a female figure holds a Bible and a broken chain (Freedom of Religion) and is casting off her cloak (of Oppression); the fleurs-de-lis on her dress indicate Nobility and she straddles a miniature earth (Liberty of Spirit).

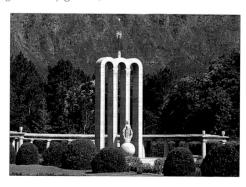

> ### SOME COMMON CULTIVARS
>
> **WHITE**
> - **Chardonnay:** the grape of the world's great white wines.
> - **Sauvignon blanc:** SA's best white cultivar, made in new world and French styles.
> - **Chenin blanc:** versatile workhorse making a range from dry to botrytis dessert wines. Also called Steen.
> - **Colombard:** easy drinking varietal, also used for brandy.
> - **Muscat d'Alexandre:** sweet, heavy mainly dessert wines. Also called Hanepoot.
>
> **RED**
> - **Cabernet Sauvignon:** this classic varietal is widely planted. New and old world styles are made.
> - **Pinotage:** SA's 'own' varietal achieving fame worldwide.
> - **Shiraz:** known for its fine flavour and 'smoky' bouquet.
> - **Merlot:** Gaining strength as a stand-alone varietal.
> - **Cinsaut:** Used mainly for blending or light easy wines.

FRANCHHOEK FOOD

- **Haute Cabriere:** offer gourmet lunches.
- **La Maison de Chamonix:** on the Chamonix estate; French food; Sunday buffet; picnics on the lawns.
- **La Petite Ferme:** simple, country-style fare (fresh or smoked trout a speciality) and spectacular views of the Franschhoek Valley.
- **Le Ballon Rouge:** French food, using the freshest of home-grown ingredients.
- **Le Quartier Français:** award-winning restaurant serving a blend of Cape Malay and Provençal dishes in a simple but elegant setting.
- **Monneaux:** tranquil setting; voted as one of South Africa's best restaurants.
- **Polfyntjies:** country-style Cape and other dishes served in a garden setting.
- **The French Connection:** well-priced French cooking. (See page 120 for contact details of the above.)

Above: *Franschhoek's early settlers remembered.*
Below: *Strawberry fields.*

The museum, a leading centre of research into Huguenot origins and culture, houses antique Cape furniture, silverware and early farm implements. Many Afrikaans surnames like Jordaan, Le Roux, Malan and Theron can be traced here.

Franschhoek, set among the vineyards of the lovely valley, is a pleasant little town that draws its prosperity from the surrounding wine and fruit farms (the area gave birth to South Africa's flourishing fruit export industry and it is part of the **Four Passes Fruit Route**, see panel, page 98). It is also a culinary mecca, its award-winning restaurants catering for a devoted clientele of national and international gourmets.

Food and wine, too, are good reasons for visiting nearby **Boschendal**, a graceful, old Cape Flemish style mansion and centrepiece of extensive vineyards. The restaurant is famed for its traditional Cape buffet lunches; the old taphouse (taphuis) serves as a tasting room; much of the rest of the house is of museum standard. On offer are tours of the estate, picnics, wine tastings and sales.

Boschendal is a member of the **Vignerons de Franschhoek**, an association established to promote the area's wines and wineries. Some may be visited by appointment only, but all their products can be sampled at the co-operative wine centre in town. Wineries include:

Bellingham, an old (1693) farm that suffered decades of neglect, is now one the region's most respected wine producers. Its cellar complex is especially impressive (wine tastings are provided); concerts are sometimes staged in its intimate (90-seat) amphitheatre.

Cabrière Estate, overlooking the Franschhoek valley, specializes in the production of Cap Classique, the name by which the Cape's sparkling wines made in the champagne method are known. The underground cellar is worth a visit.

L'Ormarins is a stunningly attractive gabled house overlooking a large ornamental pond. The cellar is old and atmospheric, its equipment high-tech.

La Motte, another estate that can trace its origins to the Huguenots, produces red wines of excellent quality.

Franschhoek Vineyards Co-operative produces wine from grapes supplied by its members, mainly under the La Cotte label. Some of the profits have been devoted to the restoration of the La Cotte mill, built in 1779. Tours are arranged by appointment.

Franschhoek Mountain Manor is a luxury hotel and conference centre, while the buildings of the adjacent **Swiss Farm Excelsior** time-share complex are designed in Alpine style, with sloping roofs, quaint weather vanes and bright-flowered window boxes.

SOMERSET WEST ★★

This fast-growing town occupies the southern part of the Stellenbosch winelands, flanked by **False Bay** and the lofty **Hottentots Holland** mountains in the east. To cross these massive ramparts, you wind your way up the dizzy heights of **Sir Lowry's Pass**.

Among the attractions of the area is the **Helderberg Nature Reserve**, a 400ha (988-acre) expanse of heath and indigenous forest (yellowwood, stinkwood and ironwood trees are prominent) set beneath the high and often cloud-wreathed Helderberg Peak. From the summit there are spectacular views of sea and mountain, vineyards and rolling farmlands. The plant life, which includes some rare proteas, was devastated by fire in 1994, but *fynbos*' powers of recovery are legendary and the outlook is good.

Starting from the reserve's entrance are several walks, the longest leading to the lovely **Disa Gorge** where, in late summer, a profusion of wild flowers decorates the slopes. Here, too, you'll find a refreshing waterfall.

TOURING WITH A DIFFERENCE

Most visitors see the Winelands by car, on conducted tours, or on foot along some of the pleasant walking trails. There are, though, some less conventional ways of exploring this scenic and interest-filled region, among them:

• **On horseback:** a number of tour operators offer horse trail excursions. Contact Cape Town Tourism
• **By helicopter:** (with wine tasting and a lunch included); contact Civair, tel: (021) 419-5182, or Helicopters and Marine services, tel: (021) 418-0200. Some operators fly to Franschhoek and further; ask Cape Town Tourism for details.
• **By hot-air balloon:** (plus champagne) contact Wineland Ballooning, Paarl, tel: (021) 863-3192.
• **By water:** Several enterprises cater for rafting and canoeing enthusiasts, including Felix Unite River Adventures; tel: (021) 404-1830.

The Helderberg is sanctuary for an array of birds, including the protea seed-eater (a species unique to the area) and, in the higher reaches, the black eagle, peregrine falcon and mountain buzzard. Among visitor amenities are a shady picnic site, a herbarium, a restaurant, and a gift shop.

One of the country's earliest and grandest mansions also lies at the foot of the Hottentots Holland range. **Vergelegen** – the name means 'situated far away', an indication of its one-time remoteness from Cape Town – was built at staggering cost by the eccentric and spendthrift governor Willem Adriaan van der Stel in 1701, and within a few years became lavishly girded by vineyards (half a million vines were planted), orchards and pastures. Such showy wealth outraged the local farmers, who complained bitterly of unfair trading competition. More serious was Van der Stel's scandalous use of official (Dutch East India Company) money, materials and slave labour in the creation of the estate, and in due course he was removed from office.

Vergelegen, like so many other historic homesteads, suffered decades of mistreatment and neglect but was eventually bought (in 1917) and restored by the magnate Sir Lionel Phillips and his wife Florence. Thirty years later it hosted an appreciative British Royal Family, and Queen Elizabeth II visited it again in 1995. It now belongs to the giant Anglo American group, and is open to the public (09:30–16:00 daily).

The house itself is ochre-walled, thatch-roofed and splendidly gabled; the interior is light, airy, filled with fine Cape cultural heritage displays and furniture, including Bayeux tapestries and an especially beautiful teak and yellowwood screen. A fairly recent addition is

TREES OF THE HELDERBERG

The majestic yellowwood and stinkwood trees found in the **Helderberg Nature Reserve** produce close-grained timber that has been fashioned into some of the finest of Cape furniture. Most of the pieces are now valuable antiques. The two most common yellowwood species are the Outeniqua, which grows to 60m (nearly 200ft) in height, and the 'real' yellowwood, the most widely distributed. Three unrelated trees bear the name stinkwood, of which the black stinkwood is the most sought-after. The red stinkwood, or bitter almond, was used in wagon-making and for domestic purposes. The hardwood forests that once covered much of the southern coastal region were depleted by early settlers, and the species are now strictly protected.

the octagonal, four-level winery (partly underground), the first products of which were released in 1992. The surrounding grounds are a 'lotion for the eyes', their focal point the Octagonal Garden, originally used for livestock and now a fantasia of wrought-iron trellises, wide herbaceous borders and flowering plants (more than 300 kinds).

Especially notable are Vergelegen's trees, among which are five camphors planted in 1700, a rare Dawn redwood (once thought to be extinct) and what is believed to be South Africa's oldest oak. There is public access to part of the house, to the **Lady Phillips Restaurant** and **Rose Terrace Restaurant**, to the interpretive centre, the lovely Octagonal and Rose gardens and winery.

ANNUAL EVENTS	
January: The Worcester Agricultural Show. **March:** Stellenbosch Carnival. Paarl Vineyard Festival. Caledon Beer and Bread Festival. Franschhoek Jazz Festival. **April:** Nederburg Wine Auction. University Rag Carnival (Stellenbosch). Cheese Festival (Paarl). **June:** The Worcester Wineland Festival. **July:** KWV Berg River Canoe Marathon from Paarl. Franschhoek Bastille Festival. **August:** Robertson Young Wine Show.	**September:** Robertson Spring Show. Tulbagh Agricultural Show. Villiersdorp Wild Flower Show. Stellenbosch Cultural (music and arts) Festival (sometimes October). Caledon and Clanwilliam Wild Flower Show. **October:** Ceres Agricultural and Wild Flower Show. Food and Wine Festival in Robertson. Simon van der Stel Festival in Stellenbosch (founder's birthday). Stellenbosch Food and Wine Festival. Church Street Festival in Tulbagh. Whale Festival in Hermanus.

THE BERG AND BREEDE RIVER VALLEYS ★

Majestic mountain ranges flank the course of the Berg River as it winds its way to the Atlantic. For a small part of the way it graces the **Perelvallei** – the 'vale of pearls' that takes its name from **Paarl Mountain** which, with its three distinctively shaped rocks, reminded an early Dutch explorer of a cluster of pearls, especially as the dawn sunlight glistened on the rounded, mica-studded surfaces. Beneath lies Paarl, largest of the region's towns.

To the north from here is the **Breede River,** which rises in the Ceres basin to flow southeast, nurturing a countryside of vineyards and orchards.

Opposite: *Vergelegen, home to an early Cape governor.*
Below: *The graceful Afrikaans Language Monument at Paarl.*

PAARL ★★

The town is noted for some impressive old buildings, for an 11km (7-mile) long main street ornamented with jacarandas and oaks, for its prominent role in the wine industry and its close associations with the long, and often controversial, campaign for the recognition of the Afrikaans language (taal). On the slopes of the mountain stands the **Taal Monument**, an impressive structure of three linked columns, fountain and soaring spire. Each of these elements symbolizes a debt owed by the language – to the Western world, to the slaves brought in from the East, and to Africa.

The mountain – which you can drive up via a circular road – is the centrepiece of the **Paarlberg Nature Reserve**, sanctuary for proteas and other *fynbos* plants, wild olives, orchids and patches of natural forest. Hiking paths, barbecue and picnic spots have been laid out; the small dams of the area are much favoured by serious anglers for the unusually large black bass they sustain.

On the way to the summit you will pass the **Mill Water Wild Flower Garden**. Do make a brief digression, especially if you're visiting in springtime (August and September), when great carpets of yellow, orange and red blooms cover the slopes.

From the top of **Paarl Rock** – where there's an old cannon, a beacon and a cave – one can take in the glory of the Berg River Valley, its towering walls and, in the distance, Table Mountain and the ocean.

In Taillefert Street is **Laborie**, a handsome old manor house and model wine estate that offers tours (by arrangement) and a restaurant serving classic Cape fare. Laborie is owned by the **KWV** (Ko-operatieve Wijnbouwers Vereniging), the world's largest cellar complex under one roof, whose massive wine and brandy cellar in Paarl's

---

WEAVING MAGIC

Bhabhathane is the Xhosa word for 'butterfly', symbolizing the colourful success of this self-help weaving scheme. It was launched in the mid-1980s in a desperate effort to beat the local unemployment crisis, and now turns out a range of handmade items, including runners, carpets and tapestries made from mohair and karakul wool. If you don't fancy what's on offer, just sketch your preference and the craftspersons will translate the design into a specially made woven product. You can visit the studio at the **Ikwhezi Community Centre**, Jan van Riebeeck Drive, Paarl.

Right: *The distinctively rounded bulk of Paarl Rock.*

Kohler Street lays on tastings and tours taking in the famed cathedral cellar with its vaulted roof and large wooden maturation vats. Spare a glance for the company's headquarters, the imposing **La Concorde** mansion on Main Street.

Worth part of your time is the **Oude Pastorie**, originally the church parsonage and now the **Paarl Museum**, which displays Cape furniture, silverware, copperware and relics of early colonial settlement. Other places of interest include the **Bhabhathane Community Project** (see panel, page 94), the **Afrikaans Language Museum**, as well as a number of places that children will enjoy (see panel, page 101).

Paarl also has its own **art route** which includes the Hout Street Gallery, the De Kraal Gallery, Ikhaya Arts and Crafts and the Glass Studio among others.

Paarl Winelands

The Paarl Wine Farms ★★★

Grandest of these farms is **Nederburg**, an elaborately gabled, classic Cape country homestead set in the wide, vineyard-mantled sweep of the **Klein Drakenstein** area to the east of Paarl. The old estate was taken over in 1937 by the Graue family, refugees from an increasingly hostile Germany.

The Graues, winemakers supreme, soon elevated Nederburg to the top rank of local producers. Nederburg, now owned by **Stellenbosch Farmers' Winery**, has held more than 25 of its annual wine auctions. This is South

PLACE OF GOATS

Unusual among wineland estates is **Fairview**, between the R44 and R102 near **Paarl**, which is noted not only for its wines but also for its farm animals, including a herd of Swiss Saanen goats whose milk yields a variety of fine cheeses. A unique feature is the estate's 'goat tower': a slender, two-storeyed, conical loft which the goats enter and leave via a circular, wooden outside stairway.

Among other farmyard residents are sheep, pigs, chickens, guineafowl, peacocks, pheasants and quails.

Fairview offers wine and cheese tasting, daily except Sundays, between 08:30 and 17:00 (13:00 on Saturdays).

Africa's premier annual wine event, noted as much for its sociability as for the fine and rare vintages on offer. Merchants, investors, collectors and others with invitations come from all corners to enjoy the sales, the tastings, the fashion show, the excellent lunch. During the rest of the year there are sales and tastings daily, and cellar tours (by appointment) that take in tastings and an audiovisual presentation; picnic lunches are served between November and March.

The more prominent of Paarl's wine venues include:
Avondale, on the slopes of the Klein Drakenstein Mountains, offers some of the finest wines in the Cape.
Backsberg, on the slopes of the Simonsberg, has an especially atmospheric tasting parlour and a small wine museum. Closed-circuit television helps you along the self-guided cellar tour.
Fairview has excellent vintages and is famous for its goat's cheese.
Landskroon, which is nearby, is also known for its cheeses from the estate's prize-winning Jersey cattle herd.
Zandwijk is South Africa's only kosher winery. Cellar tours by arrangement; children love to visit for the farmyard and for the donkey rides.

Below: *The Andrew Murray Monument outside the NG Kerk, Wellington.*

WELLINGTON ★

This attractive little town, just to the north of Paarl, is the centre of a flourishing wine-producing region and headquarters of South Africa's **dried-fruit industry**. If you're passing through, take time out to enjoy the lovely roses in **Victoria Park**. A number of charming Cape Dutch manor houses can be seen in the general vicinity, including **Twistniet** (the original homestead around which Wellington grew), **Versailles**, **Leliefontein** and **Welvanpas**.

The area's most striking feature is the 30km (20-mile) **Bain's Kloof Pass**, over which the R303 highway makes its way northeastward from town. Motorists en route are treated to spectacular views, and there's a pleasant picnic spot at the summit, after which you descend to the Breede River Valley through a countryside of ravines, waterfalls and the dramatic rock formations of the **Wolvenskloof** ('wolves' pass').

THE CERES AREA ★★

Named after the Roman goddess of agriculture, the pretty little town of **Ceres** lies in a mountain-fringed basin that is famous for its **fruit orchards** and yields magnificent harvests of apples, pears, peaches, nectarines, cherries and oranges. The local fruit-packing plant is the southern hemisphere's largest.

The upland air here is crisp and clean (even in high summer), the scenery superb – the backing hills, snow-clad in winter, attract skiers to their slopes. San rock paintings, farm tours, game reserves, cherry picking, fishing and horse riding are some of the other attractions. In a nutshell, Ceres is an inviting destination for the get-away-from-it-all weekender, who has a selection of reasonably priced hotels and family resorts from which to choose.

The **Transport Riders' (Togryers) Museum** has more information relating to the history of the area and displays an array of wagons, carts, equipment and utensils used by the early and ruggedly independent overland traders.

For driving interest, take the road southwest over **Michell's Pass**, a cleft in the towering and otherwise impenetrable highland range through which the main

> ### MEN WHO MADE TRACKS
>
> **Michell's Pass** is one of many remarkable engineering feats accomplished by the two Bains, 19th-century South Africa's leading roadbuilders. Between them, **Andrew Geddes Bain** and his son **Thomas** carved out some of the most challenging routes through the country's southern mountain barrier, creating highways into the great interior that are still used extensively today. They include the **Bain's Kloof**, **Michell's**, the precipitous **Katberg**, the **Prince Alfred's**, **Cogman's Kloof** and the magnificent **Swartberg** passes and the cliff-hugging Sea Point-Hout Bay route named **Victoria Drive**. The Bains had other talents, too. Andrew Geddes was a pioneer geologist, respected fossil-hunter and writer. Thomas surveyed railway lines, charted important mineral deposits and established the Orange River's potential for irrigation.

Left: *Ceres transformed into a winter wonderland.*

TOURING THE ORCHARDS

A splendid introduction to the Ceres-Tulbagh area is the **Fruit Route**, in which farmers, co-operatives, farm stalls and packing houses combine to provide an insight into an industry that produces apples and peaches, pears, cherries, nectarines and dried fruit. Tours last anything from a couple of hours to two days. A typical longer excursion will include a coach trip from the city, refreshments and lunch at a farm or hotel, visits to an orchard (there are also 'orchard trails'), a fruit-drying yard and a nature reserve, a tour of the harvesting and packing processes, and an overnight stay on a farm. Cape Town Tourism and local information offices (Ceres, Tulbagh, Wellington and Wolseley) will have details.

Opposite: *A candle-maker in action at Kleinplasie.*
Below: *Tulbagh's historic Church Street.*

road to the interior once ran. The route is marvellously scenic. Further to the east are the precipitous sandstone cliffs and ravines of the **Hex River Mountains**, a magnet for climbers and, in winter, for skiers. The valley below is broad, flat and incredibly fertile, sustaining nearly 200 farms that produce most of the country's late-maturing export grapes. The Hex River Valley is beautiful in all seasons, but especially so in autumn and early winter when the green land changes to a chequerboard of soft browns and golds.

TULBAGH ★

As attractive as Ceres, but in quite a different way, is Tulbagh, founded around the Old Church (built in 1745) to grow into a small frontier settlement of graceful public edifices and private homes. Many of these were destroyed in the great earthquake of 1969 – a rare occurrence in South Africa. The convulsion measured 6.5 on the Richter scale, shook the whole of the northern winelands and killed nine people.

In due course the historic and fragile buildings were restored – meticulously so – most of them to a pristine condition they hadn't enjoyed for generations (the once lovely façades had been ruined by decades of tasteless 'improvements'). In **Church Street** alone there are more than 30 considered important and handsome enough to merit status as national monuments.

Most notable of them, perhaps, is the **Old Church** (timber galleries, fine furniture and paintings) and other elements of the **Volksmuseum complex**. These include **Mon Bijou** (designed by the celebrated Louis Thibault, and today the home of a leading antique collector); the **Victorian House** and, especially, the **Old Drostdy**. This last served as home to the local *landdrost*, or magistrate, and is yet another Thibault creation. A superb building, splendidly furnished, it now does duty as museum (which contains early Cape domestic displays), art gallery and headquarters of a major wine company. Visitors are welcomed with a companionable glass of sherry in the old jail cells before touring the house.

WORCESTER ★

The Breede River Valley's largest town is noted mainly for its large showgrounds and museum complex, the most intriguing component of which is the **Kleinplasie Open-air Museum**. Located a short distance outside town, this is a permanent re creation of the life and times of the Dutch farming pioneers; on display are replicas of cottages and huts, horse mill, coach house, butchery, blacksmith's, domestic kitchen, wine cellar and *witblitz* ('white lightning': a lethal local concoction made of peaches) still, lime kiln, tobacco shed, milk room and much else. There is also an agricultural exhibition hall.

Kleinplasie is very much a 'living museum'; your visit is enlivened by demonstrations of wheat-milling, black-smithing, candle-making, bread-making, tobacco-rolling, coffee-roasting and other sturdy frontier skills. Seasonal programmes take in weaving, spinning, raisin-making, brandy-distilling and threshing, while a steam train takes visitors on nostalgic trips. There is also a restaurant which specializes in traditional cuisine such as *waterblommetjie bredie* and a shop which sells local delicacies such as cheeses, honey, preserves and jams as well as their home-made bread, candles, coffee and tobacco.

Other places of interest in Worcester include the **Hugo Naudé Art Gallery** which displays works of this respected South African artist, and the **Barn Art Gallery** which exhibits hand-blown glass.

Worcester lies on the edge of the Little Karoo, in a transitional zone noted for its fascinating plant life. The local flora and a wealth of other dryland species – bulbs, succulents, carrion flowers, the weird welwitschia, the *halfmens* and *kokerboom* trees among them – can be seen in the **Karoo National Botanic Garden** to the north of town. The 150ha (370-acre) area embraces a 10ha

STRONG DRINK

During the early days distilling was a popular home industry in rural villages and on farms. The rough-and-ready stills produced powerful **brandy-type liquors** variously known as *mampoer*, *witblits* ('white lightning') and *withond* ('white dog'). Basic ingredients ranged from peaches and grapes to potatoes, sugar cane, prickly pears and karee berries. The practice has all but died out – no new licences have been issued in the Western Cape for years – but it remains something of a tourist attraction in the country's northern regions (the Marico-Zeerust area boasts a **Mampoer Route** and annual **Mampoer Festival**). Early stills are on display at a number of venues, including the **Kleinplasie** complex at Worcester.

(25-acre) cultivated section where plants are grouped according to type, region and climate. The International Organization for Succulents ranks the reserve as one of the world's five authentic succulent gardens.

OVERNIGHTING IN THE WINELANDS

The region is exceptionally well served by hotels and, especially, by intimate little country lodges, some of them time-honoured farmsteads that pride themselves on their comfort, cuisine and friendly service (*see also* pages 118–119).

Stellenbosch has its delightful **D'Ouwe Werf** (*see* page 84) and, in the centre of town, the small and quite beautifully appointed **Stellenbosch Hotel** (architecture, décor and furnishings are a charming stylistic mix of Cape Dutch and Victorian; some of the rooms are furnished with antiques).

In the countryside nearby is the atmospherically English-country **Devon Valley Protea Hotel**. Popular for its terrace lunches and lovely gardens, it is a tranquil haven from which to explore the Winelands.

The historic **Lanzerac Hotel** (*see* page 88) also has its modern offerings, including luxurious suites and conference facilities. The Terrace restaurant serves light meals and is open between October and April, or you can lunch in the 'Governor's Hall' where South African and French dishes are served. A carvery lunch buffet is served from 12:00–14:00 every Sunday.

In Paarl and its surrounds you'll find luxury and superb food at the **Grande Roche Hotel** (its **Bosman's** restaurant wins a lot of honours) and at a

Left: *The splendid 18th-century Lanzerac homestead now functions as a hotel.*

number of smaller, less formal venues. Among the latter are **Goedemoed Country Inn**, a fine old Cape homestead set on a small estate graced by shady trees, smooth green lawns and beds of roses. The place, although commercially run, still has the feel of a well-loved private home; the antique-filled lounge remains a family room where guests gather in the evening to chat and sip a convivial glass of South African wine.

Similar in some respects to Goedemoed is **Mountain Shadows**, which has its own vineyard and 14 comfortable rooms divided between the old wine-cellar area, the **Jonkershuis** (traditional home of the heir to the estate) and the main house.

Roggeland Country House, overlooked by the lofty Drakenstein mountains, was built in 1778 and retains the thatch-roofed, gabled gracefulness of the original; reception rooms feature high-beamed ceilings, polished yellowwood and grand fireplaces; the cooking is cordon bleu.

Franschhoek offers many fine hotels and guest lodges such as **Le Ballon Rouge**, **Le Quartier Français** and **La Couronne**. Somerset West has the five-star **Lord Charles Hotel**, a place of elegant opulence (expanses of marble, beechwood trim, cascades of plants and lovely flower arrangements are features of the public rooms), every modern amenity and impeccable service. If your planned overnight stay is further afield, **Goudini Spa** is a refreshing stop. A few kilometres outside Worcester, it offers rondavels and flats, swimming pools, warm baths, jacuzzis and a restaurant.

<table>
<tr><td>

FUN FOR CHILDREN

- **Animalzone**, Klapmuts/Wellington (off R44), tel: (021) 875-5063.
- **Butterfly World**, Klapmuts (off R44), tel: (021) 875-5628.
- **Die Vonds Snake Centre**, Paarl/Wellington (off R45), tel: (021) 869 8309.
- **La Bonheur Crocodile Farm**, Klapmuts (off R45), tel: (021) 863-1142.
- **Tygerberg Zoo**, tel: (021) 884-4494.
- **Drakenstein Lion Park** and **Wiesenhof Game Reserve** (*see panel, page 85*).

</td></tr>
</table>

Worcester has the **Protea Hotel Cumberland.**

Ceres offers the long established **New Belmont,** representing the very best of the old-style South African hostelry, and also the cozy **Herberg** Guest House; Tulbagh has the **Tulbagh Hotel** and **De Oude Herberg**.

Left: *Emerald vineyards mantle the countryside around Worcester.*

7
A Day Away

Just about the whole of the region from Cape Town north through the Winelands, east across the mountains and up the western coastal belt is scenic, well developed for tourism, and there is a wide choice of hotels, lodges, coach and minibus excursions. Consult Cape Town Tourism (see page 122) for details. For visitors with their own transport, the options for day drives and forays are virtually limitless.

THE PENINSULA ★★★

The breathtaking coasts and countryside south of Cape Town are covered in a fair amount of detail between pages 45 and 67. For the independent motorist, two circular trips are especially recommended:

To **Cape Point** and back. This is the longer route, taking you in anticlockwise progression around the Peninsula, from the city to Sea Point's Beach Road (M6) and then along the western shoreline's Victoria Drive (M6) to Hout Bay (see page 54). If possible, spend time at the charming harbour, or at the World of Birds park. Continue via the scenic Chapman's Peak Drive (see page 55) and down into Noordhoek where you may wish to visit the local farm village. The road (M65) then cuts through a suburb called Sun Valley and takes you through the villages of Kommetjie and Scarborough and then inland across the southern part of the Peninsula until you reach the entrance to the Table Mountain National Park (see page 59), which ends at Cape Point (see page 60).

PENGUIN PARADE

Parts of the coast are home to the vulnerable **African penguin**, commonly known as the jackass penguin for its harsh, braying call. The **jackass** is one of only two species of this flightless sea bird found in SA (the other is the rare **rockhopper penguin**, which occurs only as a straggler). Among colonies accessible to visitors is that at **Boulders** near Simon's Town. The largest is on **Dassen Island**, off the western seaboard, where about 100,000 birds congregate.

Opposite: *The glory of Namaqualand in spring.*

THE BEST OF FISHING

Permits (available from most post offices) are required to fish off the coasts and to collect shellfish and bait. Individual species have catch limits (including size, number and season) which are strictly applied. The waters off **Cape Point** are renowned for their game fish, including marlin, tuna and broadbill. An excellent fishing spot is **Rooikrans**, on Buffels Bay near Cape Point, where you can cast directly into deep water for yellowtail and other species. **Kommetjie**, **Strandfontein**, **Kleinmond**, **Hermanus**, **Gansbaai** and **Pearly Beach**, **Melkbosstrand**, **Langebaan** and **Paternoster** are also recommended. Freshwater anglers also need a permit which also has restrictions. For a **fly-fishing** guide and permit, tel: 083 626 0467.

The return journey brings you down the east, or False Bay, coastline, along the M4 through Simon's Town, Fish Hoek and Muizenberg. Thereafter, follow the main highway (M3) back to the city.

The reverse (clockwise) itinerary – up the east and down the west coast – is of course just as pleasant.

The shorter circular route is a truncated version of the round trip. Head for **Hout Bay** and then, instead of carrying on along the coast, turn inland on the M63, which takes you up the exquisite Hout Bay Valley to the roundabout at Constantia Nek. Here you can either bear left onto Rhodes Avenue (still the M63) to the renowned Kirstenbosch National Botanical Gardens (*see* page 73) or continue straight on, down the Constantia Valley on the M41 – a beautiful woodland route that will bring you to the Groot Constantia (*see* page 75) turn-off on your right. Groot Constantia is a place for lingering. The Cape Dutch manor house, wine cellar and museum are open for inspection; the grounds invite the stroller and the restaurants offer fine cuisine (*see* page 76).

Travel back to the city via the main M3 highway. If you decided not to take the initial Kirstenbosch option – and if you have the time and energy – digress left onto the M63 (signpost Bishopscourt) and you'll see the verdant Kirstenbosch National Botanical Gardens just a short way along the road.

THE WINELANDS ★★★

There are numerous organized coach and minibus day drives and excursions on offer from tour operators, nearly all of whom are based in Cape Town. Alternatively,

Cape Peninsula

ATLANTIC OCEAN

Robben Island
Durbanville
CAPE TOWN   N1
Sea Point
Camps Bay
Sandy Bay
Hout Bay
N2
Chapman's Bay
Kommetjie   Muizenberg
Seal Island
N
Simon's Town
Table Mountain National Park   False Bay
Mast Bay
0   30 km
Cape of   Cape Point
Good Hope
0   15 miles

one can explore on one's own, and without too much prior planning – the entire Wineland countryside is a delight to the eye and an invitation to the inquisitive mind and taste buds. Simply wandering where the mood and moment lead will bring its rewards.

The character of the region and its principal attractions are covered between pages 79 and 101.

Among the more popular self-guided itineraries is the **Four Passes Drive**, a circular route that takes you beyond the Winelands proper, across the mountains into what is known as the **Overberg**, and then back through the beautiful fruit-growing areas of **Elgin** and **Grabouw**. Each of the passes offers superlative views.

Specifically, you follow the R310 through **Stellenbosch** (see page 81) and over Helshoogte Pass (the name means 'steep heights'); turn right on the R45 for **Franschhoek** (see page 89) and its pass to Theewaterskloof Dam, a large and attractive stretch of water that serves as both reservoir and playground for watersports enthusiasts. Then turn right onto the R231, cutting through the lofty Groenland Mountains via Viljoen's Pass; digress to the right through **Grabouw** and take time out to see something of the apple industry.

The village has a small museum devoted to the story of the fruit; visitors are welcome at the two large packing houses, though don't just pop in unannounced: rather contact the local information officer about laid-on tours. Leave Grabouw to join the main N2 highway

Above: *The beautiful Breede River Valley centres around Worcester and Robertson. This area is the origin of approximately a third of South Africa's total wine production. Seen here is the colombard vineyard of the Nuy Wine Cellar near Worcester, with part of the Langeberg Mountains in the background. The cellar produces mainly dry and semisweet white wines.*

BIG BIRDS ON VIEW

A 20-minute drive north (N7) of Cape Town, the **Cape Town Ostrich Ranch** offers a fascinating glimpse into the habits and habitat of these giant birds. Guided tours cover all aspects of ostrich breeding. (One ostrich egg equals 24 hens' eggs.) The skin is made into shoes, handbags and wallets. Tel: (021) 972-1955/1669.

Above: *The Hex River Valley's export grapes.*

WINELANDS WATERWAYS

An especially enticing way to explore the scenically lovely Breede River Valley is by raft or canoe. On offer are a number of organized one- and two-day excursions, including the Wine Route Canoeing and Rafting Adventure (October through to March), a leisurely paddle through the valley in the Worcester area. Food, wine, equipment and a guide are laid on; en route there are visits to historic homesteads, wine tastings and pleasant river-bank meals. Another Breede River trip takes you through the countryside around Swellendam to the east. Contact Felix Unite, tel: (021) 404-1830, or River Rafters, tel (021) 975-9727.

leading west over the magnificent **Sir Lowry's Pass** past Gordon's Bay and to Cape Town via Somerset West.

Other recommended routes include the **Boland** and **Hex River** circular drives. The former starts from **Paarl** (*see* page 94) to follow the road to **Wellington** (*see* page 96), **Worcester** (*see* page 99) and the delightful little town of **Villiersdorp** before returning to Paarl via **Franschhoek** (*see* page 89). The latter begins at **Ceres** (*see* page 97) and heads northeast on the R46, looping to the southeast to join the N1 highway to **Worcester** and the **Karoo National Botanic Garden** (*see* page 99), continuing on to **Rawsonville** and **Goudini**, the latter known for its hot springs, and then back to **Ceres** via the stunningly scenic Mitchell's Pass (*see* page 97).

Special-interest Routes

A number of thematic itineraries have been charted, giving the visitor a balanced choice of general and special-interest destinations.

These include the **fruit routes**, among which **Ceres** (*see* page 97) features prominently; the Breede River and Four Passes fruit-ways are also worth exploring.

The **Cheese Route** leads you to select dairy farms (some of which are also wine farms) which produce distinctive cheeses. Some wine estates also serve delicious cheese platters.

Among other specialized itineraries are the **French Huguenot Farms**, the **Arts and Crafts**, and the **Antiques routes**. Covering a wider area are the **Wreck Route** along the south and west coasts, the **Crayfish (rock lobster) Route** along the west coast, and the **Whale Route** stretching from the Peninsula eastwards to **Hermanus** and **Walker Bay** (*see* page 108).

Cape Town Tourism in Burg Street (*see* page 122) has full information on these, as well as pamphlets and booklets that guide you to the best bird-watching spots, to the historic lighthouses, and to places where you'll see fine displays of the Western Cape's unique *fynbos* and wild flowers.

THE SOUTHERN SEABOARD ★

The 120km (75-mile) route from Cape Town to the quaint seaside centre of **Hermanus** is a scenic delight.

Beyond **Somerset West** the marine drive cuts through coastal mountains to the picturesque village of **Gordon's Bay**, popular among Capetonian weekenders, upcountry holiday-makers and affluent owners of second homes. Private yachts and commercial fishing boats bob companionably together in the harbour; sun-lovers make for the soft sands of Bikini and Main beaches, and sporting anglers for the open sea, where fine catches of tuna and yellowtail are routinely recorded.

Deep-sea fishing boats are available for charter, pleasure cruisers and paddle-skis for hire. The small village is known for its speciality shops (hand-knitted Kei carpets are a feature), its Van Riebeeck Hotel and its splendid holiday resorts.

Gordon's Bay is one of a number of pleasant little resort centres along this stretch of the southern coast. To the south are tranquil and unspoilt **Pringle Bay** and **Betty's Bay**. The nearby Harold Porter Botanic Gardens is famed for the rich beauty of its wild flowers (the ericas are especially noteworthy) and its entrancing waterfall.

Kleinmond, at the mouth of the Palmiet River, is a holiday centre with all the amenities and a relatively wind-free climate. A variety of water birds congregate in their thousands on the lagoon and marsh lands, and in

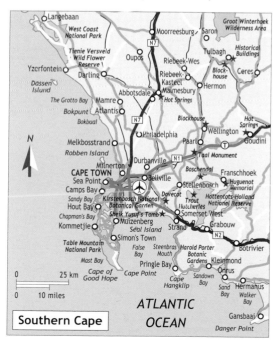

Southern Cape

WATCHING THE WHALES

From July to about November, whales can be seen sporting in the inshore waters along the coast from **St Helena Bay** to **Mossel Bay**. The best of the viewing sites, though, is the stretch from **False Bay** to **Hermanus**. Whale-watchers from all over the world gather on the cliff-top above Hermanus during the season. The giant marine mammals enter the bays both to mate and, after a year-long gestation period, to calve.

Today the total southern right population visiting the country's waters is estimated at about 2000, and the number is growing at a healthy 7% a year. Other occasional sightings include the humpback whale, Bryde's whale and the killer whale. Contact South African Tourism, tel: 083 910 1028, or Hermanus Tourism, tel: (028) 312-2629.

Below: *The picturesque harbour of Gordon's Bay.*

the Kleinmond Coastal and Mountain Reserve, which is also sanctuary to more than 1500 plant species.

The little village of **Botrivier**, a short distance inland, is the centre of a thriving wild-flower industry, its most colourful product the salmon-pink Bot River protea.

HERMANUS ★★★

The town, nestled between the mountains and the blue waters of **Walker Bay**, is one of the Western Cape's premier holiday spots and a magnet for whale-watchers. During the autumn and winter months these giant marine mammals, most of them southern rights, come inshore. One can't get too close – local conservationists make sure of that – but there are good views (through the telescope provided, but bring binoculars as well) from the high cliffs above the bay. An official 'whale crier', complete with uniform and horn, announces the arrival of these leviathans.

For the rest, Hermanus offers fine beaches, safe bathing and surfing, splendid opportunities (along the rocky coast to either side and in the placid Kleinriviersvlei lagoon) for yachtsmen, for fishermen and for divers in search of juicy crayfish (rock lobster) and *perlemoen* (abalone). Recommended is the walk along the cliff tops, and the **Rocky Mountain Way**, a scenic drive that slices through the hills. The local 18-hole golf course welcomes visitors, as does the nearby **Hamilton Russell estate**, which boasts Africa's southernmost vineyards (open Monday–Friday and Saturday morning for tastings and sales).

Among the town's more ambitious tourist schemes is its **Old Harbour**, preserved as a museum and a national monument to the fisherfolk of yesteryear. The work-worn little boats on view date from the 1850s to the 1960s;

CAPE TOWN
Somerset West
Gordon's Bay
Botrivier
Pringle Bay Kleinmond
Betty's Hermanus
Bay
Walker Bay

ATLANTIC OCEAN   Cape Agulhas

Left: *The Old Harbour at Hermanus, once a fishing centre and now preserved as a museum.*

scenes of the early days, when the place drew all its prosperity from the fruits of the sea, can be seen in the small stone museum building. Commercial fishermen, sporting anglers and other owners of leisurecraft, now use the splendid new marine complex. Some of the boats can be hired for deep-sea game-fishing expeditions.

OVERBERG ★★

In late Victorian times **Caledon**, in the Overberg ('beyond the mountain') region east of Cape Town, ranked as the southern hemisphere's most fashionable spa, its complex of pools, sanatorium, grand pavilion and superb **mineral springs** attracting devotees from afar. The most recent development is the Caledon Casino, Hotel and Spa, an ambitious gaming and family entertainment complex.

Much of Caledon's splendour disappeared after the devastating fire of 1946, but imaginative efforts have been made to restore the resort to its former glory. It now boasts the splendid **De Overberger Hotel**, built on the site of the old Victorian Bath, and there are a growing number of visitors who are 'taking the waters', drawn by the combination of hot springs, exercise, aroma-therapy massage and the sense of physical wellbeing these create. Aerobics, horse riding, golf, squash, bowls, tennis and walks in the lovely countryside are also part of the health-and-leisure scene.

OPEN-AIR EATING

The West Coast is famed for its seafood, freshly caught and often enjoyed in open air, no-frills restaurants noted for their wonderfully informal sociability as well as their delicious fare. Braaiing and potjiekos are features; on offer are crayfish (rock lobster), *perlemoen* (abalone), mussels, calamari (squid) and an appetizing array of line fish. Also on the menu are home-baked breads and jams.

Among the best-known of these alfresco eateries are: **Die Melkbosskerm,** at the country club, Melkbosstrand; **Die Strandloper** near Lange-baan; the **Breakwater Boma** at Saldanha Bay and, further north at Lambert's Bay, **Muisbosskerm.** The evenings can be chilly so wear warm clothing. The more exposed venues are wind-protected by 'skerms' (translated as rough fences). It is essential to make prior reservations to avoid disappointment.

Below: *The centuries-old Houw Hoek Inn, beyond Sir Lowry's Pass.*

The **Caledon Museum** is also worth visiting for its interesting Victoriana displays and its textile section.

The quickest way to get to Caledon from Cape Town is via the N2 national highway that twists its way over Sir Lowry's Pass before running eastwards through flatter terrain. If you're on an overnight visit, the **De Overberger** is the logical place to book into, but for a more cosy country stopover, you could try a venue in the attractive Elgin Valley at the foot of the pass. The **Houw Hoek Inn**, the country's oldest licensed hotel (it's been in business since 1794), is a rustic ranch-style cluster of buildings looking out onto the duck pond and lawns over which Shetland ponies, ducks and geese wander at will. Its pub is exceptionally sociable.

THE WESTERN SEABOARD ★

The Cape's west coast is very different from the southern maritime belt – dry, treeless, windy, and for the most part rather bleak. But it has its attractions, and at times and in some places its beauty as well.

The journey up the shoreline from Cape Town will take you along the R27 highway, past the fast-growing centres of **Bloubergstrand** (magnificent views of Table Mountain in the distance), **Melkbosstrand** (popular among fishermen) and **Darling** (15km; 9 miles inland, but worth visiting for its cultivated lupins and the beautiful chincherinchee members of the lily family) to the **Langebaan lagoon**.

For much of the way you're in sight of the sea and the drive is pleasant: it's a rather stark but often strikingly scenic coastline of jagged cliff and wide beach, heath and sandveld. On your left-hand side, opposite the tiny resort of **Yzerfontein**, you'll see **Dassen**, one of the region's larger and, in conservation terms, most important islands. Described by one scientist as among 'the naturalist's wonders of the world', it supports huge numbers of sea birds, serving as a breeding ground for, among others, the threatened African penguin (*see* panel, page 103), about 70,000 of which congregate on its rocky surface in February and again in September. Access is restricted, but visitors can approach by boat or book a trip to the island on a helicopter through Cape Nature Conservation.

Langebaan lagoon, 120km (75 miles) north of Cape Town, is an even more impressive bird sanctuary. The channel, which is 16km (10 miles) long and opens into **Saldanha Bay**, is both one of Africa's finest wetland areas and focal point of the west coast's tourism industry. Its shallow waters, the fringing mud and sand banks and the bay's islands and rocky shores are a magnet for great concourses of summertime migrants from the Arctic and sub-Arctic regions – and for cormorants, Cape gannets, gulls, herons, plovers, knots, turnstones, sanderlings and other species.

The lagoon is the centrepiece of the **West Coast National Park**, which embraces the **Postberg Nature Reserve** – haven for a variety of buck species and, in springtime, venue for a breathtaking fantasia of wild flowers. The Postberg, a 1800ha (4448-acre) area of coastal plain and granite outcrop, offers picnic spots and 25km (16 miles) of game- and flower-viewing roads. The lagoon is much favoured by the yachting and water-sports fraternities.

LANGEBAAN'S ANCIENT LIFE FORMS

Langebaan lagoon is rich in **fossils**. More than 200 extinct organisms, dating back to the **Pliocene period**, have been identified and provide insight into the region's life forms 14 to four million years ago. The **West Coast Fossil Park** has a variety on display.

The lagoon also sustained vast oyster colonies, later destroyed by a rise in water temperature. It is thought that about 30 million tons of oyster shells cover the lagoon's bed – valuable deposits commercially exploited by lime works.

GREEK PARADISE

Just to the north of Langebaan lagoon's entrance is **Club Mykonos**, a large, lively self-contained 'village' resort complex whose design and atmosphere owes much to the Greek Islands. Guests (and time-share owners) are housed in whitewashed, Aegean-style *kaliphas*; cobbled alleys and village squares complete the picture. There are restaurants, delicatessens, pubs, boutiques, a well-equipped gymnasium and sports centre (plus an aerobics and weight-training venue, heated pools, squash and tennis courts) and a 140-berth marina graced by colourful leisure craft. Club Mykonos was fairly recently granted a casino licence.

Left: *The Greek-style village resort, Club Mykonos.*

Below: *Colonies of sea
birds are a feature of the
west coast and its islands.*

Further up the coast, approximately 100km (62
miles) beyond **Saldanha** and best reached via the
inland route, is **Lambert's Bay**, a large fishing village
popular with casual holiday-makers. People come for
the large variety of fish and rock lobsters at **Bosduifklip**,
one of the region's open-air, marvellously rough-and-
ready seafood eateries. As for the bird life, **Bird Island**
(connected to the harbour) sustains vast colonies of Cape
gannets, cormorants, penguins, and a number of other
sea birds (in fact, more than 150 species altogether).
There are several almost-as-impressive ornithological
treasure-houses in the general vicinity. **Longvlei Dam**,
about 12km (7 miles) inland, is where flamingos gather
in their thousands.

Inland of the Western Seaboard

For the first 150km (93 miles) the national highway
(N7) leads through the **Swartland**, or 'black country'
(so named for the natural vegetation), and the
Renosterveld to the **Olifants River**. Other colours,
though, are perhaps more descriptive of the countryside. Gold for the great fields of waving wheat, for
instance, and green for the vines and orchards and
over a dozen other bountiful harvests.

Malmesbury is the region's principal town. More
noteworthy, perhaps, are **Citrusdal** and **Clanwilliam**,
set in the lushly productive Olifants River Valley.

Citrusdal is well
named: it's the centre
of splendidly exten-
sive orange groves
whose first seedlings
were nurtured in Jan
van Riebeeck's Cape
Town garden. One
particular tree (now a
national monument)
has been bearing good
fruit for the past 250
years. Washington,

Left: *Churchhaven, near Langebaan lagoon.*

Naval and Valencia oranges make up the bulk of the harvest, but the orchards also yield lemons, grapefruits and easy-to-peel hybrids. During the winter months approximately 6000 workers pick, sort and pack the golden crops, and the air is heavy with scent. The local co-operative lays on tours of its giant pack-house.

Clanwilliam is the headquarters of the country's rooibos tea industry. Again, visitors are welcome: tours of the estates and processing sheds are conducted during weekdays for tour groups of 15 and more. The programme includes an audiovisual presentation that covers the cultivation, grading and versatility of the leaf. The area is also noted for its gorgeous spring-time blooms, at their best in the **Ramskop Nature Reserve** and **Clanwilliam Wild Flower Garden** and, about 50km (31 miles) further away, in the enchanting **Biedouw Valley**. The valley's farmers are commendably aware of this precious floral heritage, and move their herds of sheep and cattle away to other pastures during the flowering season.

To the east of the two towns looms the towering **Cederberg**, a mountain range that takes its name from the rare and lovely Clanwilliam cedar tree. This is a

THE WESTERN ISLES

The tips of more than 30 submerged mountains off the region's south and west coasts are collectively known as **Guano Islands** – named for their vast deposits of bird manure, a valuable source of fertilizer that has been commercially harvested for centuries. Nearly all of them are uninhabited and serve as sanctuary for huge numbers of gulls, gannets, cormorants and other sea birds. Among the more notable of the western ones are **Bird Island** at Lambert's Bay, eight rocky islands in **Saldanha Bay**, and **Dassen Island**, southwest of Yzerfontein. Dassen, the largest, is 4.5km (3 miles) long by 2km (1.5 miles) wide, supports a lighthouse, a few buildings and numbers rock rabbits ('dassies' in Afrikaans) among its residents.

Right: *The Maltese Cross, a magnificent sculpted rock formation in the rugged Cederberg.*
Opposite: *A springtime scene near Wuppertal.*
Overleaf: *A bird's-eye view of the fair Peninsula.*

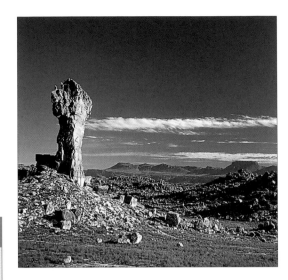

THE HEALTH-GIVING ROOIBOS LEAF

The needle-sharp leaves of the rooibos shrub, which flourishes in the uplands around **Clanwilliam**, produces an aromatic **herbal tea** that is fast gaining popularity beyond South Africa's borders (exports are even finding their way to Japan, home of perhaps the world's most discerning tea-drinkers).

For centuries the leaf has been prized for its medicinal properties, and a hot cup of the beverage certainly does have a soothing effect. There appears good reason to believe it helps relieve insomnia, nervous tension, stomach cramps, colic in babies, some allergies and, when applied directly, skin disorders such as nappy rash. A free booklet distributed to visitors gives the nutritional facts, together with rooibos recipes for soups, curries, home-made bread, punches and other drinks.

vast (71,000ha; 175,441-acre) wilderness area of starkly and often strangely eroded rock formations, of caves and overhangs, peaks, ravines, cold upland streams and waterfalls, and of magnificent vistas. The highlands are crisscrossed by some 250km (155 miles) of well-defined paths, and they attract hikers, ramblers, photographers, nature-lovers and campers from all corners. For those with energy, a couple of days to spare and a liking for great, quiet spaces, the Cederberg is an ideal destination.

NAMAQUALAND ★★★

Beyond the **Olifants River** is a dry, desolate, thinly populated region of sandveld terraces (the 'raised beaches' are relics of a time before the ocean receded) known as Namaqualand – a narrow belt of increasingly arid countryside that stretches up to the Orange River and the southern dunes of the ancient Namib Desert. Surface water is virtually nonexistent; the terrain is harsh and seldom blessed by good rains; some places record less than 50mm (2in) a year. To the casual observer, it seems that the rather arid land here cannot possibly sustain any but the toughest, least attractive life forms. But **Namaqualand**, incredibly, is home to more than 4000 floral species, most belonging to the daisy and mesembryanthemum groups, though others – aloes and lilies, perennial herbs, succulents – are well represented. The plants are resistant to drought, their seeds lying dormant just beneath the sandy surface during the long dry spells. Then, in that brief, promising period after the winter rains and before the onset of the searing desert breezes, they burst into glorious flower, transforming the countryside with great carpets of colourful blooms. Much of this region falls within the newly proclaimed (and developing) Namaqualand National Park.

This wonderful springtime show is not confined to the semiarid parts of the area. Patches of daisies and other sandveld annuals mingle with the proteas, ericas and pincushions of the Cape Floral Kingdom's *fynbos* vegetation far to the south.

The flowers are usually at their most eye-catching around mid-September, but this varies from year to year – as do the best viewing areas – according to the subtle interplay of temperature, wind and rainfall.

WATER WONDERLAND

Water-skiers rank the 18km-long (12 miles) **Clanwilliam Dam** the finest in South Africa for their sport. Moreover, it is one of the country's most attractive: the placid, ice blue stretch of water is surrounded by vineyards and lush fields of wheat, emerald green lucerne and vegetables, the whole picture framed by a stunning mountain backdrop. Yachtsmen, board sailors and powerboat enthusiasts also flock to the dam. The public resort offers self-catering chalets and caravan/camping sites with excellent facilities.

Cape Town at a Glance

Sep and **Oct** (spring): pleasant for the crisp air, and *fynbos* in flower; **Mar** and **Apr** (autumn) for balmy, still days that have lost the scorch.

A number of direct flights from most of the world's capitals land at Cape Town **International Airport**, 22km (14 miles) from the city. For more information, *see* pp. 122, 123.

An efficient **rail network** links the northern and eastern suburbs and the entire length of the eastern Peninsula with the city centre. Timetables are available at the main railway station and from Cape Town Tourism. The **Waterfront** is linked to the central area by shuttle bus. The double-decker topless **Cape Town Explorer** bus (offering two-hour tours) is an attractive way to get to know the city; contact Cape Town Tourism. **Rikkls**, inexpensive roving cabs, also cater for small groups who like to devise their own fun tours; tel: 0861 745 547. Internationally known **car hire** firms are well represented.

The following is a representative but not comprehensive selection of accommodation in and around Cape Town. A full list is available from Cape Town Tourism.

City and Surrounds
Arabella Sheraton, Convention Square, Lower Long St, tel: (021) 412-9999, fax: (021) 412-9001, www.sheraton.com/capetown Five-star with scenic views of mountain and Waterfront.
Capetonian, Pier Place, Heerengracht, tel: (021) 405-5670, fax: (021) 405-5660. Near the central area and harbour, excellent seafood.
City Lodge – V&A, tel: (021) 419-9450, fax: (021) 419-0460, www.citylodge.co.za Located at gateway to the Waterfront (walking distance from city centre).
Cullinan, Cullinan St, tel: (021) 418-6920, fax: (021) 418-3559, www.southernsun.com Located at the entrance to the Waterfront; up-market.
Dunkley House, Gardens, tel: (021) 462-7650, fax: (021) 462-7649, www.dunkleyhouse.com small, friendly but chic guesthouse in quiet central location.
Holiday Inn – Cape Town, city centre, Strand St, tel: (021) 488-5100, fax: (021) 423-1861. Linked to main shopping area by concourse; several restaurants (traditional Cape dishes, French cuisine, carvery).
Holiday Inn Garden Court – De Waal Drive, tel: (021) 465-1311, fax: (021) 461-6648. Close to Company's Garden.
Holiday Inn Garden Court – Eastern Boulevard, Woodstock, tel: (021) 448-4123, fax: (021) 447-8338. Linked to the city by a major motorway; splendid mountain views.
Mount Nelson, Gardens,

tel: (021) 483-1000, fax: (021)483-1782, www.mountnelson.co.za World renowned elegant luxury hotel; personal service, superb cuisine.
St George's Hotel, tel: (021) 419-0808, fax: (021) 419-7010. Central, on pedestrian mall.
Town House, tel: (021) 465-7050, fax: (021) 465-3891. On the fringes of the city centre; quietly tasteful.
Tulbagh Hotel, tel: (021) 421-5140, fax: (021) 421-4648. Located in attractive central city square; quiet.

Waterfront
Breakwater Lodge, tel: (021) 406-1911, fax: (021) 406-1070. Vibrant setting, good value.
The Table Bay, tel: (021) 406-5000, fax: (021) 406-5686. The ultimate in five-star luxury and comfort; excellent cuisine; superlative views over the mountain or bay; in-house spa.
Victoria & Alfred Hotel, tel: (021) 419-6677, fax: (021) 419-8955. Converted historic harbour building.

Atlantic Seaboard
Ambassador Hotel and Executive Suites, Bantry Bay, tel: (021) 439-6170, fax: (021) 439-6336, www.ambassador.co.za Spectacularly set on water's edge.
Bay Atlantic, Berkley Rd, Camps Bay, tel: (021) 438-4341, fax: (021) 438-8340, www.thebayatlantic.com One road back from the stunning Camps Bay beach.

Cape Town at a Glance

Protea Hotel President,
Bantry Bay, tel: (021) 434-
8111, fax: (021) 434-9991.
Exquisitely sited on rocky
seafront. For central
reservations for all **Protea
Hotels** tel: 086-111-9000;
www.proteahotels.com

Protea Hotel Sea Point, Sea
Point, tel: (021) 434-3344, fax:
(021) 434-3597. Near beach.

Ritz Hotel, Sea Point, tel:
(021) 439-6010, fax: (021)
434-0809. Near the seafront;
noted for revolving restaurant.

The Bay, Camps Bay, tel: (021)
430-4444, fax: (021) 438-4455,
www.thebay.co.za Splendid
luxury; spectacular sea views.

The Peninsula All-suite Hotel,
Sea Point, tel: (021) 430-7777,
fax: (021) 430-7776,
www.peninsula.co.za
Overlooks Table Bay.

**The Twelve Apostles Hotel
and Spa**, tel: (021) 437-9000,
fax (021) 437-9055,
www.12apostleshotel.com
Awesome location on coast
road between Camps Bay
and Hout Bay.

Winchester Mansions Hotel,
Sea Point, tel: (021) 434-
2351, fax: (021) 434-0215.
Family hotel on seafront.

Suburbs and Peninsula

Alphen Hotel, Constantia,
tel: (021) 794-5011, fax: (021)
794-5710, www.alphen.co.za
An 18th-century manor house.

**City Lodge – Mowbray Golf
Park**, tel: (021) 685-7944,
fax: (021) 685-7997, www.
citylodge.co.za Ten minutes'
drive from city and airport.

Courtyard Suite Hotel,
Mowbray, tel: (021) 448-
3929, fax: (021) 448-5494.
Thatched Cape Dutch home-
stead dating from 1700s.

Greenways Hotel, Claremont,
tel: (021) 761-1792, fax: (021)
761-0878, www.greenways.
co.za Private establishment;
historic Cape house.

**Holiday Inn Garden Court –
Newlands**, tel: (021) 683-6562,
fax: (021) 683-6794. Close
to Newlands rugby and
cricket grounds and
Kenilworth racecourse.

Quayside Hotel, Simon's
Town, tel: (021) 786-3838 ,
fax: (021) 786-2241.

**The Cellars-Hohenhort
Country House**, Constantia,
tel: (021) 794-2137,
fax: (021) 794-2149.
Luxury in spacious grounds.

Vineyard Hotel, Newlands,
tel: (021) 657-4500, fax: (021)
657-4501, www.vineyard.
co.za Historic country house.

Stellenbosch

Bon Esperance, Van Riebeeck
St, tel: (021) 887-0225,
fax: (021) 887-8328. Graceful
Victorian house; lovely garden.

Devon Valley Protea, tel:
(021) 865-2012, fax: (021)
865-2610. Country hotel set
amid the vineyards.

D'Ouwe Werf, Church St, tel:
(021) 887-4608, fax: (021) 887-
4626, www.ouwewerf.com
Small, historic and charming.

Lanzerac Hotel, Lanzerac St,
tel: (021) 887-1132, fax: (021)
887-2310, www.lanzerac.co.za
Gracious, historic atmosphere.

Stellenbosch Hotel, Dorp St,
tel: (021) 887-3644, fax: (021)
887-3673. Known for its
character (some parts date
back to 1743) and all-round
excellence.

Somerset West

The Lord Charles, corner
Stellenbosch and Faure roads,
tel: (021) 855-1040,
fax: (021) 855-1107,
www.nh-hotels.co.za
One of the country's best.

Paarl

Berghof, Monte Christo Ave,
tel: (021) 871-1099, fax: (021)
872-6126. State-of-the-art
guesthouse; beautiful pool.

Grande Roche, Plantasie St,
tel: (021) 863-2727, fax: (021)
863-2220, www.granderoche.
com Luxury hotel set among
terraced vineyards; plush,
international standards.

Mountain Shadows, tel: (021)
862-3192, fax: (021) 862-6796,
www.mountainshadows.co.za
Historic manor house.

Roggeland, tel: (021) 868-
2501, fax: (021) 868-2113,
www.roggeland.co.za
Historic country house set in
heart of Dal Josaphat Valley;
excellent cuisine.

Franschhoek

Chanteclair, tel: (021) 876-
3685, fax: (021) 876-2709.
Spacious grounds near town,
English country atmosphere.

Grand Province Wine Estate,
tel: (021) 876-8600 Fax: (021)
876-8601, www.grande
provence.co.za. Newly refur-

Cape Town at a Glance

bished luxury boutique accommodation and restaurant.
La Couronne, tel: (021) 876-2770, fax: (021) 876-3788.
Le Ballon Rouge, Reservoir St, tel: (021) 876-2651, fax: (021) 876-3743. Stylish and up-market.
Le Quartier Français, cnr Berg and Wilhelmina streets, tel: (021) 876-2151, fax: (021) 876-3105, www.lequartier.co.za The ultimate in luxury; superb restaurant.

Self-catering
The choice is wide, ranging from sophisticated city apartments through houses and cottages to self-contained chalets in the heart of the countryside. Contact **Cape Town Tourism**, tel: (021) 487-6800, fax. (021) 487-6899, www.tourism capetown.co.za

Budget
For **Bed and Breakfast** information, tel: Cape Town Tourism (021) 487-6800, fax: (021) 487-6899.

WHERE TO EAT

City and Surrounds
Africa Café, 108 Shortmarket St, tel: (021) 422-0221. Ethnic dishes from throughout Africa.
Anatoli, 24 Napier St, tel: (021) 419-2501. Fine Turkish fare in Middle Eastern surrounds.
Aubergine, Barnet St, Gardens, tel: (021) 465-4909. Superb service, varied menu (with emphasis on Cape and German dishes).

Bukhara, 33 Church St, tel: (021) 424-0000. North Indian cuisine; lunch and dinner.
La Brasserie, St George's Hotel, tel: (021) 419-0808. Varied menus, modern setting.
Mamma Africa, 178 Long St, tel: (021) 424-8634. African continental food, lively bar.
Maria's Greek Restaurant, Dunkley Square, tel: (021) 461-8887. Small; excellent fare.
Miller's Thumb, 10b Kloofnek Road, Tamboerskloof, tel: (021) 424-3838. Fish fare.
Rozenhof, 18 Kloof St, Gardens, tel: (021) 424-1968. Classic menu, fine food.
Savoy Cabbage, 101 Hout St, tel: (021) 424-2626. Eclectic cuisine, trendy.
The Cape Colony, Mount Nelson Hotel, tel: (021) 483-1000. Classic and Asian fusion food.
Vasco da Gama Tavern, 3 Alfred St, tel: (021) 425-2157. Portuguese, friendly, attractively down-market.

Waterfront
Shoreline Café, Two Oceans Aquarium, tel: (021) 418-8645/6. Seafood and light meals, with superb views.
Dodge City Diner, 130 Victoria Wharf, tel: (021) 418-1445. Casual 1950s style.
Ferryman's Tavern, East Pier, tel: (021) 419-7748. Converted railway shed; brewery next door; splendid beer.
Green Dolphin, Pierhead, tel: (021) 421-7471. Excellent seafood and pasta; there is live jazz nightly.

Hildebrand, The Pierhead, tel: (021) 425-3385. Popular lunch venue; dinner reservations essential, excellent service; continental cuisine.
Morton's on the Wharf, Victoria Wharf, tel: (021) 418-3633. Echoes of New Orleans, with Cajun food and blackened grills.
Panama Jack's Tavern, Elliot Basin, tel: (021) 447-3992. Informal seafood eatery.
Quay 4, tel: (021) 419-2008. Outdoor tavern downstairs, smarter upstairs
The Sea Horse Cruising Restaurant, Quay 5, tel: (021) 419-3122, www.theseahorse. co.za Wine and dine while cruising the harbour.
The Greek Fisherman, Victoria Wharf, tel: (021) 418-5411. Great calamari.

Suburbs and Peninsula
Au Jardin, Vineyard Hotel, Claremont, tel: (021) 657-4545. Elegant, French cuisine.
Bertha's Quayside Waterfront, Simon's Town, tel: (021) 786-2138, waterside dining.
Black Marlin, Main Rd, Miller's Point (near Simon's Town), tel: (021) 786-1621. Good seafood eating with bayside views.
Blues, 69 Victoria Rd, Camps Bay, tel: (021) 438-2040/1. Fine food superlatively served.
Buitenverwachting, Klein Constantia Rd, Constantia, tel: (021) 794-3522. De luxe, award-winning restaurant.
Constantia Uitsig Restaurant, Spaanschemat River Rd,

Cape Town at a Glance

Constantia, tel: (021) 794-4480.
Fine Mediterranean Provençal
cuisine, highly recommended.
Fluke's Restaurant & Bar,
Southern Right Hotel, Glen
Rd, Glencairn, tel: (021) 782-
0314. Fresh seafood served
indoors or on the terrace.
Peddlars on the Bend,
Spaanschemat River Rd,
Constantia, tel: (021) 794-
7747. Country fare, rural
surrounds, excellent value.
Red Herring, Beach Rd,
Noordhoek, tel: (021) 789-
1783. Quality fare, seafood
specialities.
Seaforth Restaurant, Seaforth
Rd, Simon's Town, tel: (021)
786-4810, seafood specialities.
Posticino, Main Rd, Sea
Point, tel: (021) 439-4014.
Classic and traditional Italian
food in the hub of nightlife.
The Brass Bell, Main Rd, Kalk
Bay, tel: (021) 788-5456. Pop-
ular with locals; overlooks the
harbour; excellent seafood.
Tides, Bay Hotel, Camps
Bay, tel: (021) 430-4444.
Innovative cuisine, elegant
atmosphere.

Franschhoek
The Cape's 'food capital'
has many fine restaurants:
Boschendal, tel: (021) 870-
4274. Cape buffet; Le Pique-
Nique among pines; Le Café.
Haute Cabriere, Pass Rd,
tel: (021) 876-3688.
Gourmet lunches.
La Maison de Chamonix,
tel: (021) 876-2393.
La Petite Ferme, tel: (021)
876-3016. Popular venue.

Le Ballon Rouge, Reservoir St,
tel: (021) 876-2651. French-
SA fusion.
Le Quartier Français, 16
Huguenot Rd, tel: (021)
876-2151. Bistro.
Monneaux, Franschhoek
Country House, Main Rd,
tel: (021) 876-3386.
The French Connection,
Main Rd, tel: (021) 876-4056,
fax: (021) 876-4036.

Paarl
Bosman's, Grande Roche
Hotel, tel: (021) 863-2727.
Gourmet cuisine.
Rhebokskloof, tel: (021)
869-8606. Wine estate
with three restaurants.

Somerset West
Garden Terrace, Lord Charles
Hotel, tel: (021) 855-1040.
Superb Cape Malay dishes,
carvery and buffet.
L'Auberge du Paysan, tel:
(021) 842-2008. Top award
winner for traditional French
fare, smart atmosphere.
96 Winery Road, tel: (021)
842-2020. Cape, Provençal
and eastern influences.

Stellenbosch
There are so many restaurants
and pubs in the town and on
surrounding wine farms – try
to obtain the free guide to the
area from Cape Town
Tourism or the Stellenbosch
Tourist Bureau and Wine
Route Office (see page 121).
De Akker, 90 Dorp St,
tel: (021) 883-3512.
Hearty pub food.

**De Oewer Riverside Food &
Wine Garden**, Aan-de-Wagen
Rd, tel: (021) 886-5431. Sister
venue of De Volkskombuis.
De Volkskombuis, Aan-de-
Wagen Rd, tel: (021) 887-2121.
Traditional Cape cooking.
D'Ouwe Werf, 30 Church St,
tel: (021) 887-1608. Cape
dishes in enchanting courtyard.
Governor's Hall, Lanzerac
Hotel, tel: (021) 887-1132.
Rather formal, very good,
splendidly historic setting.
Lord Neethling Restaurant,
Polkadraai Rd, tel: (021) 883-
8966. Splendid Cape home;
Cape and continental dishes.
The Terrace, Drostdy Centre,
tel: (021) 887-1942. Pub-style
and pizza, pleasant aspect.

TOURS AND EXCURSIONS

Canoeing in the Winelands:
Felix Unite River Adventures,
tel: (021) 404-1830, fax: (021)
670-1400, www.felixunite.com
River Rafters, tel: (021) 975-
9727, fax: 086-680-5443,
www.riverrafters.co.za
Coach tours of the Peninsula,
Winelands and West Coast:
Contact Cape Town Tourism
tel: (021) 487-6800, fax: (021)
487-6899. Hylton Ross Tours,
tel: (021) 511-1784, fax: (021)
511-2401; Windward Coach
Charter, tel: (021) 425-5440,
fax: (021) 425-5444; Specialized Tours, tel: (021) 434-
1144, fax: (021) 434-1178.
Fraser's African Destinations
(safari-type trips), tel: (021)
426-5808; Cape Options
(local hospitality tours and
services), tel: 082 873 6223;

Cape Town at a Glance

Cycle tours: Day-trippers, tel: (021) 511-4766

Helicopter trips over the Peninsula and Winelands: Civair, tel: (021) 419-5182; NAC Helicopters, tel: (021) 425-3868; Sport Helicopters, tel: (021) 419-5907; The Hopper, tel: (021) 419-8951; Executive Helicopters, tel: (021) 418-0200.

Horse trails on the beach or in the Winelands (day and overnight trails): Dunes Trails, Noordhoek, tel: (021) 789-1723; The Riding Centre, Hout Bay, tel: (021) 790-5286.

Hot-air Balloon tours: Winelands, tel: (021) 863-3192.

Steam-train trips of Winelands and wildflower regions: Computicket, see Useful Contacts.

Train trips: Rovos Rail, tel: (021) 421-4020. Long and short excursions.

Walking Tours: Table Mountain and others, Go2Africa, tel: (021) 481-4900, www.go2africa.com

USEFUL CONTACTS

Information and Publicity Offices
Cape Town Tourism, Visitor's Centre: Burg St, tel: (021) 487-6800. Information and assistance on every aspect of your visit (see page 122).

Garden Route Tourism: tel: (044) 873-6314, fax: (044) 884-0688, www. gardenroute.org.za

Hermanus Publicity Association: tel: (028) 312-2629, www. hermanus.co.za/info

Cape Town Tourism –

Muizenberg Office: tel: (021) 787-9140, fax: (021) 787-9150.

Cape Town Tourism – Simon's Town Office: tel: (021) 786-8440; Museum: tel: (021) 786-8450.

Namaqualand Tourism: tel: (027) 718-2986, fax: (027) 712-1421, www.namaqualand.com

Overberg Tourism: tel: (028) 214-1466, fax: (028) 212-1380.

Paarl Publicity Association: tel: (021) 863-4886/4937, www.paarlonline.com

Stellenbosch Publicity Association: (021) 883-3584, fax: (021) 883 8017, www. tourismstellenbosch.co.za

Stellenbosch Wine Route office: tel: (021) 886-4310, fax: (021) 886-4330, www. wineroute.co.za

V&A Waterfront Gateway Centre: tel: (021) 405-4500, www.tourismcapetown.co.za

West Coast Tourism: tel: (022) 433-8505, fax: (022) 433-8484, www.capewestcoast.org

Winelands Regional Tourism: tel: (021) 872-0686, fax: (021) 872-0534.

Other Contacts
Artscape Dial-a-Seat: theatre, opera, ballet: (021) 421-7695.

Cape Town Arts and Culture: www.tourismcapetown.co.za

Cape Town International Airport: tel: (021) 937-1200.

Castle of Good Hope: tel: (021) 787-1249, fax: (021) 787-1089, e-mail: casteel@cis.co.za

Computicket: Book for opera, theatre, ballet, concerts, sports and special events; kiosks are in selected shopping malls, or call and give your credit card number and collect tickets at venue. For credit card bookings tel: 083 915 8000; for information tel: 083 915 1234, www. computicket.co.za

Kirstenbosch Gardens: tel: (021) 799-8899, fax: (021) 797-6570; www.nbi.ac.za

Robben Island: visits and tours, tel: (021) 413-4200.

Table Mountain Cableway: tel: (021) 424-8181; weather reports: (021) 424-5148; www.tablemountain.net

Whale Hotline and Flower-line: contact South African Tourism, tel: 083 910 1028.

CAPE TOWN	J	F	M	A	M	J	J	A	S	O	N	D
AVERAGE TEMP. °C	21	21	20	17	15	13	12	13	14	16	18	20
AVERAGE TEMP. °F	70	70	69	63	58	55	54	55	57	61	64	68
HOURS OF SUN DAILY	11	10	9	7	6	6	6	7	8	9	10	11
SEA TEMP. °C	15	14	13	13	12	12	12	13	13	14	14	14
SEA TEMP. °F	59	57	55	55	54	54	54	55	55	57	57	57
RAINFALL mm	14	17	19	39	74	92	70	75	39	37	15	17
RAINFALL in	1	1	1	2	3	4	3	3	2	2	1	1
DAYS OF RAINFALL	5	4	5	8	12	12	11	13	10	8	5	5

Travel Tips

Tourist Information

Cape Town is 1402km (871 miles) from Johannesburg, 1460km (907 miles) from Pretoria, and 1753km (1089 miles) from Durban. It is is well served by international and domestic airlines and an excellent road system. Rail and passenger coach services connect the city with major centres.

Publicity Associations:
Cape Town Tourism's official Visitors' Centre is in Burg Street, near the junction with Strand Street. The Centre has a comprehensive and well-organized data bank of booklets, brochures and maps covering accommodation, places of interest, eating out, shopping, special-interest routes and much else. The Centre's complex encompasses display rooms and an Internet café, wine bar, auditorium, travel clinic and art and craft shop; trained staff handle reservations for accommodation, tours, car hire and national parks. Contact details: tel: (021) 487-6800; fax: (021) 487-6899; e mail: info@tourismcapetown.co.za website: www.tourism capetown.co.za

Open 08:30–19:00 weekdays, 08:30–17:00 Sat, 08:30–12:00 Sun.

The Tourism Gateway houses the regional offices of **Satour** (the South African Tourism Board), and information desks for the National Parks Board and the V&A Waterfront.

Entering South Africa

All visitors need passports to gain entry to South Africa. Most foreign nationals, however, are exempt from visa requirements, including citizens from Australia, Austria, Belgium, Canada, Denmark, Finland, France, Germany, Greece, Iceland, Italy, Japan, Liechtenstein, Luxembourg, Netherlands, New Zealand, Norway, Portugal, Spain, Sweden, Switzerland and USA.

Health Requirements

Visitors from or passing through a yellow fever zone must be able to produce a valid International Certificate of Vaccination. Such zones extend through most of tropical Africa and South America (air travellers in airport transit are exempt from the requirements).

Note that cholera and smallpox certificates are no longer needed, and there is no screening for AIDS.

What to Pack

Cape Town can be very hot in summer, cold and damp in

winter. Dress is generally informal; shorts, jeans and T-shirts the norm in summer (beachwear, though, is appropriate only at the beach, by the pool and on private property). Sunscreen is essential. 'Smart casual' wear is often required after dark at theatres and other venues, and by more sophisticated hotels and restaurants.

Air Travel

Cape Town International Airport is 22km (14 miles) from the city centre, accessible from the N2 national highway. **Inter-Cape** operates a shuttle between the airport and central Cape Town; car rental and taxis are available at – and some hotels provide courtesy transport to and from – the airport.

Road Travel

The region has an extensive and well-signposted network of national (prefix 'N'), metropolitan ('M') and regional ('R') highways. Surfaces are generally in very good condition.
Driver's licence: This must be carried at all times! Licences of neighbouring countries are valid in South Africa. So too are foreign licences provided they carry a photograph and are either printed in English or accompanied by an English-language certificate of authenticity. Alternatively, obtain an International Driving Permit before departure.
Insurance: Third Party cover is essential. Comprehensive car insurance is highly recommended. Rental firms will arrange such cover if you're hiring a car. Insurance tokens

are obtainable at most points of entry for overland travellers.
Petrol: Cape Town, its suburbs, the outlying centres and main routes are well provided with fuel outlets and service stations. Many of them stay open 24 hours a day; others usually from 06:00–18:00. Petrol is sold in litres; self-service is in its infancy in South Africa; pump attendants see to fuel and service needs.

Road rules and signs: In South Africa, you drive on the left; the general speed limit on major routes is 120kph (75mph), that on secondary (rural) roads is 100kph (60mph), and in built-up areas 60kph (35mph) unless otherwise indicated. Keep to the left, and pass on the right on highways with many lanes. Main roads are identified by colour signs and numbers rather than by name.
Maps: Excellent regional and city maps are available from the AA, Cape Town Tourism and bigger bookshops. Recommended are the *Globetrotter Travel Map of Cape Town*, the *Globetrotter Road Atlas of South Africa* and the *Map Studio* series.
Automobile Association: The AA of South Africa offers a wide range of services to members and members of affiliated motoring organizations. These include: assistance with breakdowns and other emergencies; insurance; car hire; accommodation reservations; touring, caravanning, camping advice; brochures and maps. Main regional office: AA House; the number for breakdowns, emergency services and lock-

smith is 083 84322, or 082 1611; Mayday medical hotline, toll free 0800 033 007.
Car hire: Major internationally known rental companies Avis, Imperial (incorporating Hertz), Budget – maintain offices in Cape Town, at the airport and at other points throughout the wider region.
Taxis: Cape Town's cabs do not cruise the streets in search of fares (nothing like London or New York). They are found in a number of designated city ranks and at several, but by no means all, suburban railway stations. Taxi companies are listed in the *Yellow Pages*. If your journey involves more than a simple, cross-city hop, ask the driver for an estimate of cost, and make quite sure he can locate your destination precisely.
Grab-a-Student, tel: (021) 448-7712, fax: 448-7714, employs students who need to earn extra money, and they drive you around in your hired car. They are more familiar with the roads, one-ways and parking areas and they are usually a mine of information on history, tourist attractions. They often speak a foreign language. (Request when booking).

There are also the **minibus taxis** that patrol the main thoroughfares and mainly travel to and from the townships. They are cheap, fast (sometimes too fast), sociable, often very crowded, and will stop if you hail them, but are not recommended for tourists. Rather call **Rikki Taxis**, a quick service which covers the central area; tel: 0861 745 547.
Buses: Regular services link the

city with all major suburbs. The main bus terminal is behind (to the west of) the Golden Acre complex.

Trains: Train services connect the city with the southern, southeastern and northeastern suburbs, but not the central and western parts of the Peninsula. The main rail terminus is on Lower Adderley Street. Criminals have been active on some stretches of the line; security has been tightened, but rather seek advice (from Cape Town Tourism or hotel reception) before embarking on trips beyond the nearer suburbs.

Accommodation

The best of the Western Cape's hotels are of an international standard. A voluntary grading system, covering all types of accommodation, is in operation; ratings range from one to five stars.Many of the better establishments are controlled by one or other of the large hotel chains; most offer packages, out-of-season, family rates and other inducements. The more prominent of the hotel groups are Sun International, Southern Sun/Holiday Inn, City Lodge (few frills, competitive rates), Karos and Protea, which is a management rather than proprietary enterprise, and its hotels have kept their individual yet professional characters.Visitors have a wide choice of **guesthouses**. (Publication available from ookshops).The outlying areas are well endowed with country getaways – restful little **lodges** tucked away in the

valleys. Most of them are supremely comfortable, some highly sophisticated in terms of appointment and cuisine; all are informal and friendly.

Guest farms are ideal for the low-cost, healthy family holiday. One stays in either the farmhouse or a chalet or cottage on the property, and takes part in the life of the ranch, farm or wine estate as the case may be.

Self-catering options throughout the wider region are numerous and varied, ranging from basic holiday apartments and cottages to well-appointed, even luxurious resort-type chalets.

Bed-and-breakfast accommodation is becoming increasingly popular, and many Capetonians are making their homes available to visitors. Ask your travel agent or Cape Town Tourism for details.

Business Hours

Normal trading and business hours are: 08:30–17:00 Mon–Fri, 08:30–13:00 Sat. Most supermarkets stay open until 19:00, later on Fridays, and on Saturday afternoons and Sunday mornings. Corner cafés and suburban mini-markets stay open from early to late every day of the week. Liquor stores close at 20:00 during the week, and 17:00 on Saturdays. No liquor sales on Sundays. Some of the malls across the Metropole offer night shopping.

Electricity

220/230 volts AC at 50 cycles/second; 15-amp 3-pronged (round pin) plugs.

Most hotel rooms have 110 volt outlets. Not all electric shavers will fit hotel and plug points; visitors should seek advice about adaptors from a local electrical supplier.

Embassies and Consulates

Most countries have diplomatic representation in South Africa, maintaining their principal offices in Pretoria. They are listed in the *Yellow Pages* (under Consulates and Embassies) and in telephone directories (listed under the country's name).

Gambling

South African gaming laws have changed radically during the past few years. Betting on horses has always been legal, but until the mid-1990s casinos were restricted to the old 'homeland' republics and national states. Currently there are more than 40 casino-entertainment-hotel complexes operating, being developed or planned in various parts of the country. Three licences have been awarded in Western Cape: one in Cape Town (GrandWest), one on the West Coast (Club Mykonos) and one in the Overberg (Caledon spa complex).

Language

South Africa has 11 official languages; those most commonly spoken in and around Cape Town are English, Afrikaans (the home language of most Coloured people) and Xhosa (the home language of most of the Cape's black residents).

Measurements

South Africa has adopted the metric system. A conversion chart appears on page 126.

Medical

Visitors are responsible for their own arrangements, and are urged to take out medical insurance before departure.

Private doctors are listed in the telephone directory under 'Medical Practitioners'.

Hospitalization is usually arranged through a medical practitioner, but in an emergency a visitor may telephone or go directly to the casualty department of a General (public) Hospital (listed under 'H' in the telephone directory).

PUBLIC HOLIDAYS

1 January (New Year's Day)
Good Friday and **Family Day** (Easter Monday)
21 March (Human Rights Day)
27 April (Freedom Day)
1 May (Workers' Day)
16 June (Youth Day)
9 August (National Women's Day)
24 September (Heritage Day)
16 December (Day of Reconciliation)
25 December (Christmas Day)
26 December (Day of Goodwill)

The Jewish, Islamic and Hindu communities observe their traditional holy days.

ROAD SIGNS IN AFRIKAANS

Altough often expressed also in English, some common Afrikaans words you'll come across include:
Links (left)
Regs (right)
Stad (city)
Straat (street)
Weg (road)
Rylaan (avenue)
Lughawe (airport)
Hawe (harbour)
Hou oop (keep open)
Gesluit (closed)
Gevaar (beware, hazard)
Verbode (forbidden)
Ompad (detour)
Tuin ('garden', but often used with 'wild', e.g.
Wildtuin – to denote a park or game reserve)
Strand (beach)
Note that, in South Africa, **Robot** is a traffic light.

Public hospitals tend to be crowded and the staff overworked (though they manage to maintain surprisingly high standards of treatment and care). Private hospitals generally offer more comfort and individual attention, but are a lot more expensive.
AIDS: The incidence of HIV infection and AIDS-related diseases has increased dramatically over the past few years and threatens to reach critical proportions. The authorities were slow to recognize the extent of the crisis, and slow to act, but they eventually launched a credible publicity and prevention programme. The risk of contracting HIV, though, is no greater in South Africa than in any other country, provided the standard precautions are taken.

Money Matters

The South African currency unit is the Rand, divided into 100 cents. Coins are issued in denominations of 1c, 2c (going out of circulation), 5c, 10c, 20c, 50c, R1, R2 and R5; while notes are available in denominations of R10, R20, R50, R100 and R200. Coinage designs have been subject to change, and some denominations circulate in two forms.
Currency exchange:
Foreign money can easily be converted into rands at banks and also through such authorized dealers as Thomas Cook and American Express.
Banks: Normal banking hours are 09:00–15:30 on weekdays and 08:30 or 09:00–11:00 on Saturdays. There are banking and exchange facilities at Cape Town International Airport. Traveller's cheques may be cashed at any bank and at many hotels and shops.
Credit cards: Most hotels, restaurants, shops, car rental companies and tour operators accept international credit cards (American Express, Bank of America, Visa, Diners Club, Mastercard). Note that

you cannot buy petrol with a credit card; most banks issue special 'garage cards'.

Value Added Tax (VAT): see Shopping.

Tipping: Provided you receive satisfactory service, it is usual to tip porters, waiters and waitresses, taxi drivers, room attendants, golf caddies and petrol attendants. Gratuities for quantifiable services (waiters, taxi drivers) should amount to at least 10% of the cost of the service; for non-quantifiable services of a minor nature (porterage, for example), it is customary to proffer plus-minus R5. Service charges: Hotels may not by law levy a charge for general services (though there is often a telephone service loading). Restaurants may levy such a charge; few do.

Newspapers

The major English-language dailies are the *Cape Times, Business Day* (morning) and *The Cape Argus* (afternoon). The latter brings out special Saturday and Sunday editions. Also available are the national weekly newspapers the *Mail and Guardian, The Sunday Times* and the *Sunday Independent,* and Afrikaans papers. Foreign newspapers are sold by selected newsagents and in some hotels.

Photography

Most international film brands and sizes are readily available in Cape Town's photographic shops and department stores; processing is generally quick

(same-day service; one-hour at some outlets).

Postal Services

Most post offices are open from 08:00–16:30 weekdays and 08:00–12:00 Sat. An international priority mail service is available. Stamps also available at CNA and some cafés and supermarkets.

Safety and Security

Do not walk alone at night; avoid deserted and poorer areas unless you're with a conducted group. Don't carry large sums of cash around with you; don't leave valuables in your room (use the hotel's security box).

Shopping

A range of necessities and luxuries is available in Cape Town. A 14% **Value Added Tax** (VAT) is levied on all sales of goods and services. This is usually reflected in the quoted price. Foreign visitors can claim back VAT paid on items that are to be taken out of the country (retain the tax invoice for this purpose).

Local products of particular interest to tourists include gold, diamond and semi-precious stone jewellery; copperware; leather (including crocodile and ostrich skin); suede goods; items made from karakul wool, mohair, ostrich feathers; ceramics; curios and African handicrafts.

Telecommunications

The telephone system is fully automatic; and one can dial direct to most parts of the world. The telephone directory lists dialling codes. Both local and long-distance calls are metred. Dial 1023 for directory queries. Fax transmission facilities are widely available. Public call boxes accept either coins or Telkom phone cards.

Time

Throughout the year, South African Standard Time is two hours ahead of Greenwich Mean (or Universal Standard) Time, one hour ahead of European Winter Time, and seven hours ahead of US Eastern Standard Winter Time.

CONVERSION CHART		
FROM	**TO**	**MULTIPLY BY**
Millimetres	inches	0.0394
Metres	yards	1.0936
Metres	feet	3.281
Kilometres	miles	0.621
Square kilometres	Square miles	0.386
Hectares	acres	2.471
Litres	pints	1.760
Kilograms	pounds	2.205
Tonnes	tons	0.984
To convert Celsius to Fahrenheit: x 9 ÷ 5 + 32		

INDEX